François Rabelais, W. F. (William Francis) Smith

# The first Edition of the fourth Book of the heroic Deeds and Sayings of the noble Pantagruel

François Rabelais, W. F. (William Francis) Smith

**The first Edition of the fourth Book of the heroic Deeds and Sayings of the noble Pantagruel**

ISBN/EAN: 9783337188894

Printed in Europe, USA, Canada, Australia, Japan

Cover: Foto ©ninafisch / pixelio.de

More available books at **www.hansebooks.com**

THE FIRST EDITION

OF

THE FOURTH BOOK

OF THE

HEROIC DEEDS AND SAYINGS

OF THE NOBLE

PANTAGRUEL

TRANSLATED BY

W. F. SMITH

FELLOW OF ST. JOHN'S COLLEGE CAMBRIDGE

LONDON

*PRIVATELY PRINTED*

1899

# PREFACE.

THE present version has been taken from my translation of Rabelais published in 1893, carefully revised with the help of the edition of M. Marty-Laveaux and the variants given in the editions of Jannet and de Montaiglon. The variants have been derived from a scrupulous collation of the copy of the Lyons edition of 1548 in the *Bibliothèque nationale*.

It was thought that readers of Rabelais would welcome a separate translation of the "rudimentary" *Fourth Book* written at Metz, which might enable them better to appreciate the position of Rabelais at this anxious period of his life, and to compare the work which he wrote in exile with the help of a few books with that which he composed in the quiet of a Benedictine house aided by the resources of a good library. The comparison again of the completed *Fourth Book* of 1552 with this fragment displays to advantage the writer's skill in addition and amplification ; considerable changes are made without impairing the dramatic features of the book or suggesting the idea of patchwork. A *motive* is also supplied for the admirable *Prologue* originally written for this instalment, but subsequently laid aside on the completion of the *Fourth Book*.

Notes have been taken in many cases from the earlier translation, but new illustrations and explanations have also been given. For the most part the present notes are explanatory and indicative of sources rather than linguistic.

The letter to the Cardinal du Bellay has been prefixed to the book.

*b*

# INTRODUCTION.

## FOURTH BOOK.

### (*First Edition.* 1548.)

RABELAIS had written his *Third Book* in the quiet and comfort of the Monastery of St. Maur des Fossés, of which he speaks so enthusiastically in his "Epistle of Dedication" of the later edition of the *Fourth Book*. On its publication at the beginning of the year 1546, although it was protected by the King's Privilege, dated September 19th, 1545, the increasing severity of the persecutions of heretics during the painful malady of Francis I. made it evident that France was no longer safe for the author of so suspected a book. Rabelais at once retired to Metz immediately after, or possibly even before, the publication of the book. He must have left Paris hurriedly and with a small equipment of books, as may be discovered by examining the composition of this first instalment of the *Fourth Book* and comparing it with the completed Book as it appeared later in 1552. An interesting letter survives addressed from Metz to Cardinal Du Bellay, and dated February 6th. By its contents and by an extract from the record in the library at Metz given in the editions of MM. des Marets and Marty-Laveaux we are enabled to decide almost, if not

quite, conclusively that the date-year was 1546. The
letter contains a piteous appeal to the Cardinal for pecuniary
help, and the extract (dated 1547) speaks of payments to
Rabelais, no doubt in the capacity of physician, of 60 *livres*
up to S. Remy (October 1st), and of 60 *livres* up to Easter,
and of 30 *livres* up to St. John's day (June 24th). In the
letter he had spoken of "taking service elsewhere, to the
detriment of his studies, unless he received immediate
help," and we may draw the inference that he did so, by
the record of these payments. To the early part of 1546 is
also to be assigned the letter of Jean Sturm, director of the
gymnasium at Strasburg, to Cardinal du Bellay, in which
occurs the following passage: "Tempora etiam Rabelœsum
ejecerunt e Gallia, φεῦ τῶν χρόνων! Nondum ad nos
venit. Metis constitit, ut audio, inde enim nos salutavit.
Adero ipsi quibuscunque rebus potero cum ad nos venerit.
. . . . Ad Tabernas Alsatiae (*Saverne*) vigesima octava
Martii."

Our Doctor then was installed as physician to the
hospital at Metz in the years 1546-7. From the Prologue
to the *Fourth Book* of 1548 we learn that he was approached
by some courtiers from Paris declaring their appreciation of
his *Third Book* and begging him to continue his writing.
This no doubt was the origin of the *Fourth Book*. In the
present instalment we find a far more sparing use of books,
especially classical books. Ovid's *Fasti*, Virgil, Homer's
*Odyssey* (no longer the *Iliad*), Pliny, Gellius, Suetonius,

Diogenes Laertius, Valerius Maximus, complete the tale of his classical sources. In this we must except the 10th and last long chapter—the 11th is but a fragment—which in 1552 was augmented and expanded so as to correspond to chapters 20-24 of Fezandat's edition (B). This chapter derives from some other sources, and may, therefore, have been partly written, as well as the Prologue, at Lyons, while the other chapters were being printed. Rabelais, we know, reached Rome about the middle of 1548 and most likely stopped at Lyons on the way, in order to see this new book through the press. Afterwards, while in attendance on Cardinal du Bellay in Rome till the end of 1550, and at Meudon from the beginning of 1551, he had plenty of books and leisure to elaborate and enlarge the eleven chapters which he had written in exile at Metz with the aid of his scanty library.

Of other books employed in this part the most considerable use is made of the macaronic poem of "Baldus" by Merlin Cocai (Theophilo Folengo), from which much had been taken in *Pantagruel* and somewhat in the *Third Book*. From this book are derived the episodes of the Sheep-dealer and Panurge, and of the Storm, altered, however, and amplified with excellent effect. In the seventh chapter (the 17th in B) are taken a couple of instances from a book by Baptista Fulgosus, or Fregoso, who was Doge of Venice (1478-1483) and a considerable author. The work in question was *De dictis factisque memorabilibus, illis exceptis quae*

*Valerius Maximus edidit*, reprinted by Galliot du Pré (Paris, 1518). Book IX, chap. 12 of this treatise supplies matter for this seventh chapter, and also later for the 33rd chapter of the completed *Fourth Book*. In the seventh chapter also occurs the death of Bringuenarilles the Giant (an account continued later in c. 44). This is borrowed from *Le Disciple de Pantagruel* a small *fabliau* of very small merit, from which two or three episodes in the *Fourth* and *Fifth Books* are taken.

Rabelais must also have consulted some book on the circumnavigation of Africa by the Portuguese, to which he had alluded before in *Gargantua*. These voyages and the explorations of the New World and the Canary Islands had engaged his attention several times in his book. One or two stories seem to come from the *Apophthegmata* of Erasmus, which was also at times a fruitful source for him.

The general impression produced by these few chapters is that when Rabelais is left more to his own resources and with fewer books, his style is, if possible, more fresh and crisp than at other times; at all events, the episodes of *les moutons de Panurge* and of the Storm, seem to be more widely appreciated than most of the other parts of his writings.

# BIBLIOGRAPHY

### OF

## *THE FOURTH BOOK.*

### EDITIONS PRINTED WITH RABELAIS' AUTHORITY.

A. 1548. Issued at Lyons without 'the printer's name, but probably from the press of P. de Tours, the successor of François Juste.

B. 1552. Printed by Michael Fezandat, Paris.

A contains the *Ancien Prologue* (as it was called when superseded by the Prologue of the completed book), and eleven chapters.

B contains an Epistle of Dedication to the Cardinal of Châtillon and a New Prologue, both of which derive something from the *Ancien Prologue.* The eleven chapters of A are added to and amplified so as to extend to twenty-five chapters, while some few omissions in this part are made in B, mostly from prudential motives, to avoid offence to the Theological faculty. The completed book extends to sixty-seven chapters.

In the last nine leaves of B are a number of explanatory notes, entitled *Briefve déclaration d'aucunes dictions plus obscures contenues on quatriesme liure des faicts & dicts Heroïcques de Pantagruei.*

### EXPLANATION OF REFERENCES.

A. P. F. = *Anciennes Poésies Françaises du xv$^{ème}$ et xvi$^{ème}$ siècle,* par A. de Montaiglon.

ℜ = *Roman de la Rose* ed. Francisque Michel.

References are given to *Garg.* and *Pant.* instead of to books i. and ii., because it appears certain that the book *Pantagruel* was written before *Gargantua.*

# LETTER

## TO THE CARDINAL DU BELLAY.[1]

MY LORD,

If M. de Saint-Ay, on coming here lately, had had the Advantage of taking Leave of you at his Departure, I should not now be in so great Necessity and Anxiety, as he will be able to explain to you more at large. For he assured me that you were well minded to give me some Alms, provided that he could find a trusty Man coming from your parts. Indeed, my Lord, unless you take Pity on me, I know not what I am to do, unless in the Extremity of Despair I take Service with some one about here, to the Detriment and evident Loss to my Studies. It is not possible to live more frugally than I do, and you cannot make me so small a Gift from the abundance of

1 M. des Marets, who gives this letter (preserved in MS. at Montpellier, among the Latin and French letters to and from Cardinal du Bellay) has been at pains to look for other correspondence between Rabelais and this Cardinal, but with a negative result.

He also gives an extract taken from the library at Metz: " 1547 payé à Mre. Rabellet p. ses gages d'un an, c'est à sçavoir à la Saint-Remy 60 livres, à Pasques darien passé 60 livres, comme plus c'on lui ont p. le quart d'an de Saint Jean 30 livres."

M. de Saini-Ay is mentioned elsewhere as one of the gentlemen attached to the Seigneur de Langey. His name was Orson Lorens. iv. 27.

Goods that God hath placed in your Hands but that I can
manage by living from Hand to Mouth, and maintain
myself honourably, as I have done up to the present, for
the Honour of the House from which I came on my
Departure from France.

My Lord, I commend myself very humbly to your kind
Favour, and pray Our Lord to grant you a very happy and
long Life with perfect Health.

Your very humble Servant,

FRANCIS RABELAIS, Physician.

From Metz this 6th of February (1546).

# THE FOURTH BOOK

### OF THE

# HEROIC DEEDS AND SAYINGS

### OF THE NOBLE

# PANTAGRUEL

#### COMPOSED BY

# MASTER FRANCIS RABELAIS

### DOCTOR IN MEDICINE

### AND CALLOÏER OF THE ISLES OF HYERES

——: o :——

## AT LYONS

THE YEAR ONE THOUSAND FIVE HUNDRED AND FORTY-EIGHT

# PROLOGUE[1] OF THE FOURTH BOOK.

DRINKERS very illustrious, and you, gouty Tasters[2] very precious, I have seen, received, heard and understood the Ambassador[3] whom the Lordship of your Lordships hath despatched towards my Paternity, and he hath appeared to me a very good and eloquent Orator.

The Summary of his Proposition I reduce to three Words, which are of so great Importance that formerly among the Romans by these three Words[4] the Praetor made Answer to all Requests set before him in Judgment ; by these three Words he decided all Controversies, all Complaints, Processes and Differences ; and those Days were styled unlucky and *nefasti*,[5] on which the Praetor did not use those three Words ; *fasti* and lucky, on which he was wont to use them.

You *give*, you *say*, you *adjudge*. O good People, (I cannot see you![6]) may the worthy Powers of God be to you, and not less to me, eternally for a Help ! So then, from God be it ; never let us do anything, that His most holy Name be not first praised.

---

1 This Prologue was suppressed in the Paris edition of 1552, and in its stead appeared the " Epistle dedicatory " to the Cardinal of Châtillon, and the New Prologue, which contained parts of this.

2 Fr. *goutteurs*, an equivoque between *goûter* and *goutteux*.

3 *The Ambassador* refers to the gentleman who was sent by several courtiers to present to Rabelais a silver wine-flask in the form of a breviary (Cf. *Garg.* 5. 41) addressed possibly with some phrase like *au très révérend Père, etc. . . , d. d, d,* etc., accompanied by some appreciative remarks on his former writings. The priestess Bacbuc

makes Panurge drink out of a similar *book* (v. 46).

4 *Do, dico, addico Do* (actionem), *dico* (tutorem pupillo), *addico* (bonorum possessionem).

5 Ille nefastus erit per quem tria verba silentur :
Fastus erit per quem lege licebit agi.
Ovid, *Fast.* i. 47.

6 *I cannot see you.* Cf. *Pant.* 3, iv. N. Prol. M. Heulhard, who interprets the " Lordship of your Lordships " to be the King himself, takes the expression " I cannot see you " here quite literally, to the effect that Rabelais, being at Metz, could not see the courtiers who were in Paris.

You *give* me. What? A fine and ample Breviary. In very Sooth, I thank you for it; this will be the least of my greatest Efforts.[1] What kind of Breviary it was, certainly I did not think, as I looked upon the Book-marks, the Rose, the Clasps, the Binding and the Covering, in which I have not omitted to consider the Hooks and the Pies[2] painted thereupon and placed in mighty fine Array; by which, as though they were hieroglyphic Letters, you tell me plainly that there is no Work like that of Masters, nor Courage like that of Lick-spigots.

To lick the Spigot signifieth a certain Jollity, metaphorically extracted from the Prodigy which came to pass in Brittany a short time before the Battle that was fought near St. Aubin du Cormier.[3] Our Fathers have told it us; it is right that our Successors should not be ignorant of it. It was the Year of the good Vintage;[4] a Quart of good and dainty Wine was sold for a one-tagged Point.

From the Countries of the East flew thither a great Number of Jays on one side, and a great Number of Pies[5] on the other, all making for the West; and they went alongside one another in such Order, that towards the Evening the Jays retreated to the left—understand here the [a]lucky Side in Augury—and the Pies to the right, near enough to one another. Through whatever Region they passed, there remained no Pie which did not ally itself to the Pies, nor Jay that did not join the Camp of the Jays. So they went on and on flying, till they passed over Angers,

a Cic. *de Div.* ii. 39, § 82; Serv. ad Verg *Aen.* ii. 693.

1 Fr. *le moins de mon plus* (iii. 5). Cotgrave translates this: "The most I can, the least I should."

2 Fr. *crocs et pies* = hooks and magpies, so forming *crocquer pie* by a rebus.

3 *St. Aubin du Cormier.* A battle took place here, July 28, 1488, between King Charles VIII. and the Duke of Orleans, afterwards Louis XII, who was taken prisoner. Cf. *Garg.* 50.

4 We learn from the *Contes d'Eutrapel*, c. 23, that there was a great vintage in Anjou about this time, when wine was practically given away.

5 A combat between jays and pies is recorded by Poggio in his *Facetiae* (No. 234) under the title *Pugna Picarum et Graculorum*, on the confines of Brittany in April 1451. This one has been placed in 1488 just before St. Aubin du Cormier.

a Town in France that bordered on Brittany, in Numbers so much multiplied, that in their Flight they put out the Brightness of the Sun from the Lands subjacent.[1]

In Angers at that time was an old Gaffer, Lord of Saint-George, named Frapin ;[2] he it was who made and composed the fair and joyous Carols in Poitevin Language. He had a Jay, a great Favourite by reason of his Chatter, by whose means he invited all Visitors to drink ; he never sang of anything but Drink, and he called him his Chatterbox ; this Jay in martial Fury broke out of his Cage, and joined the other Jays as they went by. A neighbouring Barber, named Gapechat, had a female Pie of his own, a very gay Bird ; she by her Presence increased the Number of the Pies, and followed them to the Combat. Here be Matters mighty and paradoxical, true notwithstanding, witnessed and avouched. Note well everything. What came of it? What was the End?

What came of it, good People? A marvellous Result! Near the Cross of Malchara[3] took place the Battle, so furious that it is horrible only to think of it. The End was that the Pies lost the Battle, and on the Field were cruelly slain to the number of 2,589,362,109, besides[b] Women and little Children, that is, besides Females and little Pies: that you understand. The Jays remained Victors, not however without Loss of several of their good Soldiers, whereby there was very great Damage throughout the Country.

b Matt. xiv. 21.

1 This expression seems to be borrowed from the report brought to Leonidas at Thermopylae, that the arrows of the Persian host were so numerous that they obscured the sun, when he replied : " All the better; we shall fight in the shade." Plut. *Ap. Lacon.* 225 B., Val. Max. iii. 7, 8.

2 *Frapin.* M. des Marets acutely suggests that this may mean Lucas *Le Moyne*, the author of some *Noëls* in 1520 (reprinted 1860), Frapin and Frappart (iv. 15), being sobriquets of monks.

3 *Malchara.* This allusion has not been explained fully. There is a Hosanna Cross at St. Maixent in Poitou mentioned in iv. 13, n. 12; and in the *Contes d'Eutrapel*, c. 19 (*ad fin.*), there is mention of " la journee de *Marhara* . . . une brave composition *entre les pies et les geais*, qui s'y pelauderent tant brusquement."

The Bretons are a brave Folk,[1] as you know ; but if they had understood the Prodigy, they would easily have recognised that Ill-luck would be on their side ; for the Tails of the Pies are in Shape like their Ermines,[2] while the Jays have in their Plumage some Resemblance to the Arms of France.[3]

To our Subject. Chatterbox returned three Days later, quite woebegone and wearied out with these Wars, having one Eye knocked out ; however, a few Hours after he had fed at his old Commons he recovered his good Spirits. The fashionable Folk, the People, and the Scholars of Angers ran together in Crowds, to see Chatterbox the one-eyed thus accoutred. Chatterbox invited them to drink, as was his wont, adding at the End of each *Invitatorium:*[4] " Eat Pie." I take it for granted that that was the Watchword on the Day of the Battle ; all did their Duty therein. The Pie of Gapechat never returned ; she had been eaten. From this arose the proverbial Saying that to "*Drink Healths and with great Draughts*" is verily *To eat the Pie.*[5] With such Figures, for a perpetual Memorial,[6] Frapin had his Dining-Hall and lower Hall painted ; you may see them at Angers on the Terrace[7] of Saint-Lawrence.[8]

---

1 Fr. *gens*, with an equivoque on *gents*.
A Delleveu bretons sont gens,
Mais il y en a de dou père.
     *Les menus propos*, l. 415,
          A.P.F. xi. p. 383.

2 *Ermines*, the arms of Brittany.

3 *Arms of France.* Jays have in their plumage blue and white, the azure and argent of the French arms.

4 *Invitatorium*, the refrain of the invitatory, 94th Psalm, *Venite exultemus* at Matins, in the Breviary.

5 Fr. *crocquer la pie* has been variously explained. *Pie* seems to be akin to *piot*, and connected with πίνειν. The expression itself occurs in the *Nef de santé* (Paris 1507), and in the old *Farces* and *Sotties*.
     Galans, allons *croquer la pie* ;
     Je n'en puis plus si je ne *pie*
     Quelque pianche bonne et freche.

6 Papal bulls often concluded their first sentence with the words : *ad perpetuam rei memoriam.*

7 Fr. *tartre* = modern *tertre.* The *tertre Saint Laurent* still exists in Angers.

8 There is a story of a raven in the time of Tiberius something like this, in Pliny, x. 43, § 60, and of a still more wonderful bird in Plutarch, *de Soll. An.* c. 19, 973 C-E. Cf. also Petronius c. 28, *fin.* super limen cavea pendebat aurea in qua pica varia intrantes salubatat.

This Figure engraved on your Breviary made me think
that there was somewhat more than a Breviary. Moreover,
with what Purpose should you make *me* a Present of a
Breviary? I have, thanks to God and you, some old ones,
aye and new ones too. Upon this Doubt, on opening the
said Breviary I perceived that it was a Breviary made by
mirific Invention, and the Book-marks all to the point, with
appropriate Inscriptions.

Therefore your Wish is that at Prime I should drink
white[1] Wine, and also at Tierce, Sext and Nones; at
Vespers and Compline Claret (red) Wine. That you call
*Eat the Pie*; verily never were you[c] hatched by an evil Pie.  c Cf. v. 6.
I will therein *grant* your Request.

You *say*. What? That in no Respect have I galled
you in all my Books heretofore printed. If on this Subject
I quote for you the Sentence of an old Pantagruelist, still
less shall I gall you :

> It is (he says) no common Praise
> To have the Art the Court to please.[2]

Moreover, you say that the Wine of the Third Book
hath been to your Taste, and that it is good. True it is,
there was but little of it, and what is commonly said : "*A
little and good*" is not to your liking ; more to your liking is
what the good Evispan of Verron[3] used to say : "*Much and
good.*" Over and above this, you invite me to the Con-
tinuation of the Pantagrueline History, alleging the Utility
and Enjoyment derived from the Reading of it among all
worthy People, and excusing yourselves for not having been

---

1 *White wine*, etc.. with reference to the proverb:
  Rouge le soir, blanc le matin
  C'est la journée du pélérin.
2 Principibus placuisse viris
  non ultima laus est.
    Hor. *Epp.* i. 17, 35.

Quoted by Erasmus, *Adag.* i. 4, 1.

3 *Evispan of Verron.* Verron
was a tract of land near Chinon.
Cf. "*Multi bonique*," Erasm. *Ad.*
i. 6, 31.

obedient to my Prayer,[1] containing the Request that you should reserve your Laughter till the seventy-eighth Book.

This I pardon you with all my Heart: I am not so churlish or implacable as you would think; what I was saying to you was not for your Hurt; and by way of Answer I speak to you in the Vein of Hector's Speech put forth by Naevius, that *'Tis a fine Thing to be praised by praiseworthy Folk*.[2]

By a reciprocal Declaration I say and maintain, as far as to the Fire exclusively[3]—understand this and for a Reason —that you are fine honest People, all descended from good Fathers and good Mothers; at the same time promising you on the Word of a Foot-traveller,[4] that if ever I meet you in Mesopotamia, I will use my Influence with the little Count George[5] of Lower Egypt that he shall make a Present to each of you of a fine Nile Crocodile and a Nightmare[6] from the Euphrates.

You *adjudge*. What? To whom? All the old Quarters of the Moon to the Cowl-pates, Vermin, Ape-faces, Booted Monks, Hypocrites, Frieze Coats, Hairy-paws, Mumping Pardoners, Sham-saints. These be fear-inspiring names,[7] only in hearing the Sound of them; at the pronouncing

1 *Prayer*, in allusion to the request at the foot of the title-page of the Third Book: *L'autheur susdict supplie les lecteurs benevoles soy reserver à rire au soixante et dixhuytiesme livre.*

2 The line is from the *Hector Proficiscens* of Naevius:
Laétus sum laudári me abs te,
    páter, a laudató viro,
and it is quoted three times by Cicero (*Tusc. Disp.* iv. § 67, *ad Fam.* v. 12, § 7; xv. 6).

3 Fr. *jusqu'au feu exclusivement.* Cf. *Pant. Prologue.*

4 Fr. *foy de pieton*, a parody of *foy de chevalier.*

5 *Count George* probably refers to a visit of some " Bohemians " to

Paris, mentioned by Pasquier in his *Recherches*, iv. 19. He speaks of " douze pénitenciers qui vinrent à Paris le 17 août 1427, c'est à savoir, un duc, un comte et dix hommes, lesquels étaient de la Basse Egypte, et qui devaient par pénitence aller sept ans parmi le monde."

6 Fr. *Cauquemare*, properly night-mare; here and in iv. 64 it is used of a fabulous animal. *Pant. Prol.* 6.

7 *Cowl-pates*, etc. These names of abuse for the monks and friars may be found in i. 54, ii. 34, iv. 32 and 64. *Pant. Prog.* 5.
Nomina sunt ipso paene timenda sono.—Ovid, *Her.* xiii. 54.

thereof I have seen the Hair of your noble Ambassador stand on End on his Head. I have only understood the High Dutch of this, and I know not what sort of Beasts you comprise in these Denominations. Having made diligent Research in divers Countries, I have not found a Soul who acknowledged them, or who endured to be thus named or designated. I take for granted that it was some monstrous Kind of barbarous Animal in the time of the tall Bonnets;[1] now it has died out in Nature, just as all sublunary Things have their End and Period, and we know not what is the Definition thereof; for you know that when the Subject is lost its Denomination also is easily lost.

If by these Terms you understand the Calumniators of my Writings, more aptly you may call them Devils, for in Greek Calumny is called *diabolè*. See how detestable before God and the Angels is this Vice styled Calumny— that is, when a man impugns good Action, when he speaks ill of good Things—for it is after this and not after any other Vice (though several might seem more enormous) that the Devils of Hell are named and called. These Persons are not, properly speaking, Devils of Hell; they are their Apparitors and Ministers; I style them Devils, black and white, Devils private, Devils domestic; and what they have done towards my Books they will do, if they are permitted, towards all others. But it is none of their Invention. I say this, to the end that they may not hereafter glorify themselves with the Surname of the old Cato the Censor.

Have you ever heard what is meant by "spitting in a Bason"?[2]

Formerly the Predecessors of these private Devils, Architects of Sensuality, Subverters of Decency (like a

1 Fr. *les Hauts Bonnets*. Ridiculous head-gear *temp*. Louis xi.
2 Fr. *cracher au bassin* (*Garg.* 11, *Pant.* 12), a proverbial expression of those who contribute unwillingly under stress of public opinion, etc. Rabelais here takes it literally.

Philoxenus[1] or a Gnatho and others of a like Kidney) in the Wine-shops and Taverns, in which Places they ordinarily kept their Schools, seeing the Guests served with some good Meats and delicate Morsels, would villainously spit in the Dishes, so that the Guests, disgusted at their infamous Spittings and Snivellings, might abstain from eating the Meats set before them, and the Whole might be left to these villainous Spitters and Snivellers.

Almost like, not however so abominable, is the Story[2] we are told of the fresh-water Physician, Nephew of the Advocate, the late Amer, who said that the Wing of a fat Capon was bad, the Rump doubtful, the Neck good enough, provided the Skin had been taken away; to the end that the Patients should not eat thereof, but that all should be reserved for his own Mouth.

Thus have done these new Devils in Frocks. Seeing all this World in eager Appetite to see and read my Writings, on account of the preceding Books, they have spit in the Bason; that is to say, they have by their Handling bewrayed, decried and calumniated them all; with this Inten-

---

1 *Philoxenus* is the glutton mentioned by Athenaeus (viii. 26, p. 341 A) and Aristotle (*Eth. Nic.* iii. 10, 10; *Eud.* iii. 2, 12) as wishing for a neck longer than a crane, so as to get more taste from his food.

*Gnatho* is the parasite in Terence's *Eunuchus*, whence the name is generic.

Rabelais has in his mind the passage in Plutarch, *Mor.* 1128 A, where he relates that Philoxenus and Gnatho were so greedy that they thrust their noses into dishes, that they might eat the whole themselves, by disgusting other guests. Sir T. Browne, in a grave discussion on Philoxenus, quaintly puts it that this second Philoxenus "was so uncivilly greedy, that to

engross the mess, he would preventively deliver his nostrils in the dish" (*Pseud. Ep.* vii. 15).

2 This story, as well as the preceding one, is repeated in v. Prol., the doctor's precept being given in a mock hexameter:

Ala mala, cropion dubium, collum bonum pelle remota.

*Amer, physician of sweet water.* Confusion is purposely introduced in this passage in order to contrast *amer* (bitter) with *doulce* (sweet), a real "salt" with a fresh-water sailor, and *eau douce* with *urine*, which was much regarded as a test by physicians, and in order to bring in the allusion from *Patelin* (745).

Je retourneray, qui qu'en grousse
Cheuz cest *avocat d'eaue douce* (*i.e.*, briefless).

tion, that none should heed them, none should read them,[1] save their own Poltroonities. I have seen this with my own Eyes—it was not with my Ears;—nay, they go so far as to preserve them religiously during their Offices at Night, and employ them like Breviaries for use by day; they have taken them from the Sick, the Gouty and the Unfortunate, to cheer whom, in their Discomfort, I had made and composed them.

If I could take under my Care all those who fall into Infirmity and Sickness, there would now be no Need to publish and to print such Books. Hippocrates has made a Book for this Purpose, which he has entitled, *On the State of the Perfect Physician*[2]—Galen has illustrated it with learned[d] Commentaries—in which he orders that there be nothing in the Physician (he even goes so far as to particularise the Nails) which can offend the Patient. Everything that is in the Physician, Gestures, Face, Clothing, Words, Looks, Touch, is to please and delight the Sick man.

For my Part and in my homely Fashion, I do strain and strive to do this as regards those whom I take under my Care. So do also my Companions on their part; wherefore, perchance, we are called Parabolani[3] with the long

d xvii. b. 145 K.

---

1 Fr. *ne les eust, ne les leust, fors leurs Poiltronitez*, used in contradistinction to *ma Paternite* above.

2 There are two such treatises, which have been attributed to Hippocrates and which practically form one, Περὶ Ἰητροῦ and Περὶ Εὐσχημοσύνης. The passage, however, occurs in Hipp. *Epidem*. vi. (Kühn, vol. iii. pp. 603, 624. This is repeated in the *Epist. Ded.* of this book in B.

3 *Parabolani* were a kind of nurse-doctors, so called from their practice of recklessly (like *enfans perdus*, παράβολα, Plin. *Epp*. ix. 26, § 4) tending patients afflicted with every kind of disease. They are mentioned in Justinian's Code i. tit. 3, l. 18, *de episc. et cleric*., as numbering more than 600 in Alexandria in Egypt (Cf. Gibbon, c. 47, n. x.) Accursius in his Gloss on Dig. xxvii., following the grammarian Modestinus, seems to have given a definition *parabolani sunt medici* which greatly offends our Doctor. Cf. Cael. Rhod. xxix. 11.

Sleeve[1] and the large Elbow,[2] according to the Opinion of two Scavengers, as foolish in Interpretation as it was dull in Invention.

There is a further Point. On a Passage of the Sixth Book of the *Epidemics* of the said Father Hippocrates, we labour in Disputation, not if the Countenance of the Physician when moping, sour, morose, disagreeable, downhearted, depresses the Patient, and the Countenance of the Physician when joyful, serene, pleasant, smiling, open, elates the Patient—that is all proved and certain—but whether such Depressions and Elations proceed from Apprehension of the Sick man, on contemplating these Qualities, or whether it is by Transfusion of the Spirits, serene or gloomy, joyous or sad, from the Physician to the Patient, as is the Opinion of the Platonists and the Averroists. Since, then, it is impossible that I can be called in by all the Patients, that I can take all Sick folk in my Charge, how envious it is to take from those who are languishing and sick the Pleasure and joyous Pastime—without Offence, be it said, to God, the King, or any other—which they find in my Absence, in listening to the Reading of these joyous Books!

So then, since by your Adjudication and Decree these Slanderers and Calumniators are seised and possessed of the old Quarters of the Moon, I forgive them.

There will be no laughing hereafter for all, when we shall see these lunatic Fools, some Lepers, others Bulgarians, others a Cross between Lepers and Bulgarians,

> Dashing and smashing and gnashing their Teeth,
> Breaking the Windows all about Town,
> Hang themselves, drown themselves, fling themselves down,

---

1 Fr. *focile*, the greater of the two bones between the elbow and the wrist.

2 Fr. *code*, with a poor pun on *code* and *coude*, the elbow. Rabelais is alluding to the *philonium* or ancient robe of the physicians. Cf. *Ep. ded.* It had four sleeves, two of which reached to the hands, and the other two hung from below the elbow.

and speeding full Gallop to all the Devils, according to the Energy, Faculty and Virtue of the Quarters which they shall have in their Noddles, be they waxing, beginning, gibbous,[1] horned[2] or waning. Only, towards their Malignities and Impostures I will employ the Offer which Timon the Misanthrope did to his ungrateful Athenians.

[e] Timon, angered at the Ingratitude of the Athenian people towards him, came one day into the Public Assembly of the City, requesting an Audience to be given him for a certain Business concerning the public Good. At his Request Silence was made, in expectation of hearing things of Importance, seeing that *he* had come to the Assembly, who so many Years before had absented himself from all Company and lived in his own Privacy. Then he said to them :

         [e] Plut. Anton. c. 70 ; Shakesp. Timon, v. i., 208. Erasm. Apoph. v. (Timon, 11).

"Outside my private Garden, under the Wall, is a spreading, fine and remarkable Fig-tree, · on which you Gentlemen of Athens when in despair, Men and Women, Young men and Maidens, are accustomed to go aside and hang and strangle yourselves. I give you Notice that, for the Convenience of my House, I am purposed within a Week to destroy the said Fig-tree. Wherefore, whoever of you and of all the City wishes to hang himself, let him make all Haste to do so. When the aforesaid Term has expired, they will have no Place so fitting, and no Tree so convenient."

Following his Example, I announce to these diabolical Calumniators that they have all to hang themselves within the last Quarter of this Moon ; I will furnish them with Halters ; I assign to them for a Hanging-ground the Place

---

1 Fr. *amphicyrces* should be *amphicyrtes* (ἀμφίκυρτος). This refers to the shape of the moon on her 11th and 19th day. Cf. Macrob. *in Som. Sc.* i. 6, § 55.

2 Fr. *brisants*. According to Ménage, this is the shape of the moon on her 4th and her 26th day. Cf. v. 23.

between Mid-day and Faverolles.[1] After the New Moon they will not be taken in there so cheaply, and will be obliged, themselves, at their own Expense to buy Cords, and to choose a Tree for their Hanging, as did Mistress Leontium, the Calumniator of the most learned and eloquent Theophrastus.[2]

1 *Mid-day*, etc. A grotesque jumbling of time and place. There are several places in France named Fevrolles (cf. v. 26, n. 2).

2 " Adversus Theophrastum, hominem in eloquentia tantum ut nomen divinum inde invenerit, scripsisse etiam feminam, et proverbium inde natum suspendio arborem eligendi." Plin. *Praefat.* § 27 (Sillig). Cf. Cic. *de Nat. Deor.* i. 33, § 93.

Rabelais is in error explaining the somewhat confused statement of Pliny. Erasmus puts it correctly: " In re vehementer indigna neque ullo pacto toleranda, veteres arborem suspendio deligendam esse dicebant. Inde natum quod olim in Theophrastum philosophum praecipuum meretricula nomine Leontium ausa sit scribere." (*Adag.* i. 10, 21). Corn. Agrippa *de van. scient. c.* 63. Cael. Rhod. *Ant. Lect.* x. 8. Cf. ταῦτα δῆτ᾽ οὐκ ἀγχόνη; (Arist. *Ach.* 125). Quamobrem elegit suspendium anima mea, et mortem ossa mea.—Job. vii. 15.

# CHAPTER I

## How Pantagruel put to Sea to visit the Oracle of the Holy Bacbuc.[1]

In the Month of June, on the Day of the [a]Feast of Vesta[2]—the very Day on which[b] Brutus conquered Spain and subjugated the Spaniards, on which also[c] Crassus the covetous was defeated and conquered by the Parthians— Pantagruel taking leave of the good Gargantua his Father (the latter praying devoutly for the prosperous Voyage of his Son and all his Company), put to Sea at the Port of Thalassa, accompanied by Panurge, Friar John of the Trencherites, Epistemon, Carpalim, Gymnast, Ponocrates,[3] Rhizotomus and others, his Servants, Domestics and Old friends, together with Xenomanes,[4] the great Traveller and Traverser of perilous Ways, who had arrived certain Days beforehand, at the[d] Summons of Panurge.

[a] Ov. *Fast.* vi. 247-50.
[b] Id. vi. 1-2.
[c] Id. vi. 465-6.
[d] iii. 49.

The Number of the Ships was such as I have set forth to you in the *Third Book*,[5] well rigged, caulked and stored, and well furnished with great abundance of *Pantagruelion*.

1 *Bacbuc* is a Chaldæan word, signifying Bottle. It occurs several times in the O.T.

2 The 9th of June.

3 In B Ponocrates is omitted, probably by accident, as he appears in iv. 9, 22, 63 of that edition. He appears in *Garg.* but not in *Pant.*

4 Xenomanes is identified with Jean Bouchet, a friend and correspondent of Rabelais, by a volume of poems published by him under the title *Opuscules du Traverseur des voies perilleuses*(4°,Jac.Bouchet, Pictavii, 1526).

5 We are told in iii. 49 that they were twelve in number, like the contingent of Ajax at Troy.

The Meeting-place of all the Officers, Interpreters, Pilots, Skippers, Midshipmen, Rowers and Sailors, was on board the Thelamane;[1] for that was the Name of Pantagruel's great Flagship; and she had on her Stern for Ensign a large and capacious Bottle, half of Silver, smooth and polished; the other Half was of Gold, enamelled with crimson Colours; whereby it was easy to determine that White and Claret were the Colours of the noble Travellers, and that they were going to get the Word of the Bottle.

On the Stern of the Second was carried aloft a Lantern of antique Shape ingeniously made of speculary Stone,[2] to denote that they would pass by Lantern-land.

The Third for its Device had a fine deep Ewer of Porcelain ;

The Fourth a golden Jar with two Handles, as though it were an antique Urn ;

The Fifth a famous Tankard of Sperm of Emerald ;[3]

a *Garg.* 8 *fin.*    The Sixth a monkish Drinking-horn made of the[a] four Metals ;

The Seventh a Funnel of Ebony embossed all over with Gold in enamel Work ;

The Eighth a Goblet of Ivy, very precious, damascened with beaten Gold ;

The Ninth a Wine-cup of rich refined Gold ;

The Tenth of aromatic Agalloch (you call it Wood of Aloes) purfled with Cyprus Gold of Persian work ;

---

1 *Thelamane* is superseded in B by *Thalamege,* which was the name of the Egyptian galley on board which Cleopatra took Julius Cæsar on a trip to Aethiopia. Cf. Suet., i. 52.

2 *Lapis specularis* = talc. Plin. xxxvi., 22, § 45.

3 Pliny's *smaragdus Cyprius* (xxxvii. 5, § 17) is the *smaragdo prase,* or *plasma di smeraldo* of the Italians. (Italis *Prasma,* Emeraude brute. Ducange).

The Eleventh a golden Vintage-basket made in Mosaic-work ;

The Twelfth a Runlet of dead Gold, covered with a scroll of small Indian Pearls in arabesque Work.

In such wise was it that there was no one, however sad, sour or melancholy, nay, had it been Heraclitus the Weeper, who did not feel unwonted Delight and smile with lightened Spleen,[1] as he looked upon this noble Convoy of Ships and their Devices ; who did not say that the Travellers were all honest Topers and jolly good Fellows, and who did not judge with sure Prognostication that the Journey both in going and returning would be performed in Mirth and perfect Health.

In the Telamonie then was the general Meeting. There Pantagruel made them a brief and pious Exhortation, wholly backed by Authorities taken from Holy Writ, on the Subject of Navigation. When this was ended, common Prayer was made to God in high and clear Tones in the Hearing and Understanding of all the Burgesses and Citizens of Thalassa,[2] who had flocked to the Mole to see their Embarkation.

After the Prayer there was melodiously chanted the ᵃPsalm of David, which begins : a Ps. cxiv.

When Israel went forth out of Egypt, &c.

When the Psalm was finished, the Tables were spread on the Deck, and Meats speedily served. The Thalassians,

---

1 Cor sapit et pulmo loquitur, lel commovet iras ; *splen ridere facit*, cogit amare jecur. Ebrard *Graecismus*, c. xix. 106.

2 *Thalassa* (θάλασσα) Sea, is chosen as the name of the port from which the fleet starts.

who likewise had chanted the aforesaid Psalm, had Store of
Victuals and Wine[1] brought out of their Houses. All
drank to them ; they drank to all.

This was the Reason why not one of the Assembly was
sick from the Rolling of the Sea, nor was troubled at all in
Head or Stomach; which Inconveniences they would not
so comfortably have prevented by drinking Water some
days before, either salt or fresh, or mixed with Wine ; or
by taking Pulp of Quinces, or Lemon-peel, or Juice of
sour-sweet Pomegranates ; or by keeping a long Fast; or
by covering their Stomach with Paper,[2] or by using other
Remedies which foolish Physicians prescribe for those who
put to Sea.

After often renewing their Tipplings, everyone retired to
his own Ship, and in good Time they set sail to the Greek
Wind[3] as it got up, to which Point the chief Pilot had
shaped their Course and set the Needles of all their
Compasses.

For his Advice, and also that of Xenomanes, was—seeing
that the Oracle of the Holy Bottle was near Cathay in
upper India—not to take the ordinary Route of the Portuguese,[4] who, sailing through the Torrid Zone and the Cape
of Bonasperanza at the south Point of Africa, beyond the
Equinoctial Line, and losing the Sight and Guidance of the

1 A: *vinaigre*, B : *vinage*. This
must be a misprint in A.
2 Against sea-sickness the German Emperor advised a strong
*bouillon* "such as the English
love," and firm bandages round the
stomach. (Sept. 1897).
3 Fr. *vent Grec* (*vento Greco*),
N.E. wind.

4 *Portuguese.* From the time of
Prince Henry the Navigator, the
Portuguese had gone on tenta-
tively coasting round Africa. In
1487 Bartholomew Diaz rounded
the Cape of Good Hope ; in 1498
Vasco da Gama sailed round Africa
as far as Melinda (*Garg.* 5) and
from there crossed over to India.
(Cf. *Pant.* 24).

Arctic Pole, make an enormously long Voyage ; but to follow, as near as possible, the Parallel of the aforesaid India and to tack to the westward of that Pole,[1] so that, winding under the North, they might be in the same Latitude as the Port of Olonne,[2] without coming nearer it, for fear of coming into and being shut up in the Frozen sea. And following this regular Turn by the same Parallel they might have the Eastward on their Right, which at their Departure was on the Left.

Now this turned out to their incredible Advantage ; for without Shipwreck, without Danger or Loss of Men, in great Calm, they made the Voyage to Upper India in less than four Months, which the Portuguese could scarcely do in three years, with Dangers innumerable. And I am of this Opinion, that some such Route was perhaps followed by the Indians who sailed to Germany and were honourably treated by the King of the Swedes at the time when Q. Metellus Celer was Pro-consul in Gaul, as hath been described to us by Cor. Nepos and Pliny after him.[3]

---

1 *Follow the Parallel, &c.* This refers to the famous North-West passage.

2 *Olonne* is the sea-port of Talmont in Poitou (*Garg.* 16).

3 Q. Metello Celeri . . . Galliae proconsuli Indos a rege *Suevorum* dono datos . . . Nepos tradit, qui ex India commerci causa navigantes tempestatibus essent in Germaniam abrepti.    Plin. ii. 67, § 67.

# CHAPTER II

## How Pantagruel met a Ship with Travellers returning from Lantern-Land.

THAT Day, and for the two Days following, they neither sighted Land nor saw anything new, for they had formerly ploughed the Main on this Route. On the fourth Day[1], as we were already beginning by degrees to wind about the Pole, going farther from the Equinoctial, we discovered a Merchant-vessel making sail towards us on the port Side. The Joy was not small on our part as well as on that of the Merchants; with us, in getting News from the Sea; with them, in getting News from *Terra firma*.

As we came in with them, we discovered that they were Frenchmen from Saintonge. While we discoursed and reasoned together, Pantagruel learned that they came from Lantern-land, whereat he found a new Accession of Joy; as did also the whole Fleet, especially when we enquired as to the Condition of the Country and the Manners of the People of Lantern-land, and being advertised that at the End of the following July[2] was fixed the Meeting of the Chapter-general of the Lanterns, and that great Preparations were being made as though they intended to lanternise there profoundly.

1 B c. 5 has "On the *fifth* Day."
2 The sixth session of the Council of Trent was appointed to be held on the 29th of July, 1546.

While we were hearing this News, Panurge got up a
Quarrel with a Merchant of Taillebourg,[1] named Dindenault,
who had on board the Vessel a great Number of Sheep.

The Occasion of the Quarrel was on this wise.  This
vain-glorious Dindenault, seeing Panurge[a] without a Cod-    a Cf. iii., 7.
piece and wearing Spectacles on his Bonnet, said to his
Companions concerning him : " See there a fine Figure for
a Cuckold."

Panurge, by reason of his Spectacles,[2] heard more clearly
with his Ears than usual.  So then, hearing this Remark,
he asked the Dealer : " How the Devil could I be a
Cuckold, who am not yet married, as thou art, as I can
discern by thy ill-favoured Phiz ?

" Yea, verily," answered the Dealer, " that am I, and
would not be otherwise for all the Cod-pieces in Asia and
Africa ; for I have in marriage one of the prettiest, gentlest,
honestest Women in all the Country of Saintonge, with the
good Leave of all the others ; and I am bringing to her
from my Travels a fine eleven-inch Branch of Coral as a
Christmas-box.  What hast thou to do with it ?  Wherein
wouldest thou be meddling ?  Who art thou ?  Whence art
thou ?  Thou Spectacle-wearer of Antichrist, answer, if
thou art of God."

1 Taillebourg a small town on the
Charente in Saintonge 6 miles N. of
Saintes.

The celebrated story of "Panurge
and the Sheep " is taken from Merlin Cocai ; in the 11th book of the
macaronic poem of *Baldus* is an
account of Baldus, Cingar (the pro-
totype of Panurge), and Lonardus
getting on board a vessel in the
Adriatic at Chioggia with some
Ticinese sheep-dealers, with one of
whom Cingar has a deal and a

quarrel resembling this episode in
many points.

2 Cf. iii. 35, and  Hudibras iii.
3, 13.
Sets up communities of senses
To chop and change intelligences ;
As Rosicrucian virtuosos
Can see with ears, and hear with
    noses.

Cf. Shaks. *Mids. N.* iii. 1, 93 ;
iv. 1, 209 ; v. 1, 194 ; Aesch.
*P. V.* 21.  *S. c. T.* 100.

"I demand of thee," said Panurge, "if with the Consent of all the Elements I had biscoted thy Wife in such wise that the stiff God of the Gardens, Priapus, who dwelleth here in free Quarters, all Subjection to Cod-pieces being removed, had remained in her Body in such Disaster that he would never come out, but remain there for ever, unless thou shouldest draw him out with thy Teeth, what wouldst thou do? Answer, thou Cod-piece-wearer of Mahomet, since thou art of the Devil's Gang."

"I would give thee," answered the Dealer, "a Sword-stroke on this spectacled Lug of thine, and would slay thee like a Ram."

As he said this, he was drawing his Sword; but it stuck in the Scabbard, for you know that at sea all Harness easily takes Rust by reason of excessive Moisture.

Panurge ran off to Pantagruel for Help. Friar John put his Hand to his Cutlass and would have slain the Dealer outright with it, had it not been that the Master of the Ship and some of the Passengers besought Pantagruel that an Outrage might not be committed aboard his Vessel,[1] whereupon all their Difference was settled, and Panurge and the Dealer shook Hands and pledged each other
b Cf. iii., 41    heartily in Drink in token of [b]perfect Reconciliation.

1 Baldus ut audivit bravamina scoriat ensem,
Nam sibi displicuit villanos esse superbos.
Cingar eum tenuit dicens: mihi, deprecor, istam

Desine vindictam . . . . .
. . . . . . . . . . . . .
Baldus ei paret, fodroque recondidit ensem.
Merl. Coc. xi. 116-122.

# CHAPTER III

## HOW PANURGE CAUSED THE SHEEP TO BE DROWNED AND THE MAN WHO WAS IN CHARGE OF THEM.

The Quarrel being quite appeased, Panurge said secretly[1] to Pantagruel and Friar John :

" Withdraw yourselves here a little out of the way and pass your Time merrily in what you shall see. There will be rare Sport, if the Rope do not break."[2]

Then he addressed himself to the Dealer and drank to him over again a full Cup of good Lantern Wine ; the Dealer pledged him gaily in all Courtesy and Honesty.

That done, Panurge besought him earnestly of his Goodness to consent to sell him one of his Sheep.[3]

The Dealer answered him : " Alas, alas, my Friend, my Neighbour, how well you know how to put your Tricks upon poor Folk. Verily, you are a rare Customer. Oh, you mighty Sheep-buyer ! In good sooth you have the Cut, not a bit of a Sheep-buyer, but rather of a Cutter of Purses. By St. Nick, what a rare Thing it would be to carry a full Purse in your Neighbourhood at a Tripe-house in a Thaw[4] !

1 Clugar cum tenuit dicens: mihi, deprecor, istam Desine vindictam ; nunc nunc miranda videbis: Est villanorum toleranda superbia nunquam. Altri ridebunt, altri sed forte piangent. Merl. Coc. xi. 118-121.

2 *i.e.* unless my plot falls through. A metaphor from a swing.

3 Fraudifer ergo loquit pastorem Cingar ad unum : Vis, compagne, mihi castronem vendere grassum ? Merl. Coc. xi. 130-1.

4 In a tripe-house in a thaw, tripe would be sold very cheap, and cutpurses would make a rare harvest in the crowd of would-be purchasers. cf. Winter's Tale iv. 4, 616. Et vont à Saint-Marcel as tripes, ℛ 5774.

Ha, ha! how you would get over any one who did not know you! But haw, haw! only look, good People, how he has the Cut of an Historiographer."[1]

"Patience," said Panurge. "But to the point; as a special Favour sell me one of your Sheep. How much?"

"What do you mean, my Friend, my Neighbour?" answered the Dealer. "These be—

> Sheep of the long-woolled kind[2]—Jason took from them the Golden Fleece; the Order of the House of Burgundy[3] was derived from them—
>> Sheep of the East,
>> Sheep of high Breed,
>> Sheep of high Feed."

"I believe you," said Panurge; "but prithee sell me one, and for a Reason, if I pay you well and on the Nail, in Money of the West, of low Breed and of low Feed. How much?"

"My Friend," answered the Dealer, "my Neighbour, of the Fleece of these Sheep will be made the fine Cloths of Rouen; the fine Cloths made from the Bales of Limester,[4] in comparison with it, are mere Flock. Of their Skin will

---

1 *Historiographer*, a royal chronicler or literary person provided with a pension. Probably a jeering reference to the long brown toga and spectacles of Panurge. Cf. iii. 7.

2 *Long-woolled sheep* Fr. *moutons à la grande laine* (*Garg.* 8, 53; iii. 2) were old gold coins bearing the figure of Christ as the *Agnus Dei*, worth about 16 fr. They dated from the time of St. Louis.

3 *i.e.* the *Toison d'or*, instituted by Philip the Good, Duke of Bur-

gundy in 1429, with the idea of the achievement of the Golden Fleece by Jason.

4 *Limester* (prob. = Leominster). Cf. *Friar Bacon and Friar Bungay* (Dodsley viii. p. 220):
> Yielding forth fleeces stapled with such wool
> As *Lempster* cannot yield more finer stuff,
and
>> far more
> Soft than the finest *Lemster* ore.
> Herrick *Hesperides*, 443.

be made fine Morocco Leather, which will be sold for Morocco from Turkey, or from Montelimart, or from Spain at the worst. Of the Guts men will make Violin and Harp Strings, which will be sold as dear as if they were Strings from Monaco. What think you?"

"If you please," said Panurge, "you will sell me one; I shall thereby be very much beholden to you, even to the Knocker[1] of your Door. See here is Money down. How much?"

This he said showing his Purse full of new Henricuses.[2]

"My Friend," answered the Dealer, "my Neighbour, they be Meat for none but Kings and Princes. Their Flesh is so delicate, so savoury and so dainty, that it is like Balm. I bring them from a Country in which the Hogs (God be with us!) eat nothing but Myrobalans, and the Sows are fed only with Orange-flowers."

"But," said Panurge, "sell me one of them, and I will pay you like a King, on the Word of a Pawn."[3]

"My Friend," answered the Dealer, "our Neighbour, these be Sheep bred from the very Race of the Ram that carried Helle over the Sea called Hellespont. Over all the

---

1 *Even to the Knocker*, probably referring to some feudal service, but there are traces of it in Greek literature. Cf. Eur. *Ion.* 1612.

νῦν δὲ καὶ ῥόπτρων χέρας ἡδέως ἐκκρημνάμεσθα καὶ προσεννέπω πύλας.

Also Lysias *in Andoc. ἀσεβείας* p. 103. Xen. *Hellen.* vi. 4, 36.

2 *New Henricuses.* Henry II. had recently come to the throne. These coins were put into circulation by an order bearing date Jan. 31, 1548 (Heulhard). They were *douzains* (*duodenarii.*) On one side the shield of France between two crescents with the imperial crown over them and with the inscription Henricus II., &c. On the other side was a cross made of 8 crescents ending in fleurs de lys, and two H's between the arms of the cross, with the inscription *Sit Nomen Dei benedictum* (Ducange).

3 Fr. *foy de pieton* (=*pion* foot-soldier) opposed to *foy de chevalier.*

Fields where they pass, the Corn grows as if the Lord had
passed there ; there needs no other Tillage or Manure.  Besides this, from their Urine the Quintessentials extract the
best Saltpetre in the World; with their Dung (so please you)
the Physicians of our Country heal seventy-eight kinds of
Diseases, the least of which is the Evil of St. Eutropius of
Xaintes,[1] from which God save us and keep us.  What
think you, our Neighbour, my Friend ?   Also they cost
me a good Price."

"Muck, muck," said the Master of the Ship to the
Dealer ; "there is too much Haggling here.  Sell him one
if thou wishest ; if thou dost not wish, do not play the
Fool with him."

" I will do so," answered the Dealer, "for Love of you ;
but he shall pay me three Livres of Tours for each,[2] taking
his Choice."

"'Tis a great deal," said Panurge ; "in our Country I
could have five, nay six, for such a Sum of Money.  See
whether it be not too much.  You are not the first Man I
have known who in wishing to become rich too soon and to
make his way, has fallen backwards, nay sometimes broken
his Neck.[3]  Well, hold, there is your Money."

Panurge, having paid the Dealer, chose out of the whole
Flock a fine big Sheep, and carried him off crying and

---

1 *Evil of St. Eutropius* = dropsy.
Cf. *Garg.* 45.  Igni sacro medetur
oesypum.   Plin. xxx. 12.
2 Sum contentus ego, vendam,
    pegorarius inquit:
    Da mihi quinque tronos (7 fr.
    50 c.) si vis, aut quattuor ad
    plus.
        Merl. Coc. xi. 133-4.
3  'ruit in se magna frequenter

Progenies, et quo petit altius, icta
   ruinam
Deterius capit, ac proprio fert
   damna flagello.
        Merl. Coc. xviii. 14-16.
Semper ero . . . . contrarius am-
   bitiosis
Qui possint utinam medium sibi
   rumpere collum.
        Id. xii. 269-70.

bleating, all the others seeing and hearing and bleating in
concert, and staring to see which way their Companion was
being led.

Meantime the Dealer was saying to his Shepherds : " Ah!
how well my Customer knew how to choose ; the Whoreson
has skill in Cattle.  Honestly, truly and honestly, I was
reserving that one for the Lord of Candale,[1] well knowing
his Disposition ; for by Nature he is quite merry and over-
joyed when he holds a good-sized, tempting Shoulder of
Mutton in one Hand, like a left-handed Racquet, and with
a good sharp Carver in the other, God knows what a Knife
and Fork he plays."

All at once, I know not how, the Affair was so sudden
that I had not Time to consider it, Panurge, without saying
another Word, throws his Sheep crying and bleating into
the Middle of the Sea.[2]

All the other Sheep, crying and bleating in like Tone,
began to throw themselves and leap into the Sea after him
in a String.  There was a great Crush as to which should
leap first after their Leader.  It was impossible to keep
them from it ; for you know that it is the Nature of the
Sheep always to follow his Leader, wherever he may go.

The Dealer, quite scared at seeing his Sheep perish and

1 *Candale*, a misprint in A for
*Cancale* (B).  Cancale is a seaport
in Brittany, three leagues E. of St.
Malo celebrated for oysters and
good cheer.

2 Cingar per binas castronem
  brancat orecchias.
Quem buttat in medio cernen-
  tibus aequora cunctis.
Illico (nam mos est ovium
  seguitare priorem)

Omnis grex sequitur, praeceps-
  que nodare caminat
Postque caporalem certatim
  mandra ruinat,
Immo gaudenti cantabant car-
  mine bè bè.
      Merl. Coc. xi. 143-148.

Cf. Dante *Purg.* iii. 79-84.  *Con-
vito* i. 11.  Erasm. *Ad.* iii. 1, 95.

drown before his Eyes, strove to keep them back with all
his Might ; but in vain. They all leaped into the Sea one
after another and perished.

At last he laid hold on a great, strong one by the Fleece
on the Deck of the Ship, thinking thus to hold him back,
and so to save the rest also. The Sheep was so powerful
that he carried the Dealer into the Sea with him, so that
he was drowned, in the same Manner as the Sheep of
Polyphemus, the one-eyed Cyclops, carried ªUlysses and
his Companions out of the Cave.

So did the other Shepherds and Sheep-drivers, taking
the Sheep, some by the Horns, others by the Legs, others
by the Fleece; and they were all likewise carried into the
Sea and drowned miserably.

Panurge beside the Cook-room, holding an Oar in his
Hand, not to help the Sheep-drivers, but to keep them
from climbing on the Ship and escape drowning,[1] preached
to them eloquently, as though he had been a little Friar
Oliver Maillard or a second Friar John Burgess,[2] pointing
out to them by Common-places of Rhetoric the Miseries of
this World,[3] the Blessings and Felicity of the other Life,
affirming that the Departed are far happier than those
living in this Vale of Misery, and promising to each of
them to erect a fair Cenotaph and a Sepulchre in his

1 Cingar nil ridet sed velle jutare
videtur
Atque trabuccanti pecudi suc-
currere fingit,
Sed magis in fluctus buttans
quoque clamitat oh, oh !
Merl. Coc. xi. 165-7.

2 Olivier Maillard and Jean
Bourgeois were celebrated
preachers in the reigns of Louis XI.
Charles VIII. and Louis XII.

3 Cf. *Liber de contemptu mundi,
sive de miseria humanae conditionis
ab Innocentis Papa tertio* (Coloniae
1496). Cf. also *Garg.* 42, *de contemptu mundi et fuga saeculi.* The
treatise of Innocent III. is much
employed in Chaucer's *Man of
Law's Tale.*

honour on the highest Point of Mount Cenis[1] at his Return from Lantern-land; nevertheless—in case they were not yet weary of living among Men, and so Drowning were not to their Taste—wishing them Good-fortune and that they might meet with some Whale, which on the third Day afterwards might set them ashore safe and sound in some Land of Satin,[2] after the Example of Jonah.

The Ship being cleared of the Dealer and his Sheep, Panurge said: "Remaineth there here no other sheepish Soul? I know nought therein. 'Tis a Trick of the old War. What thinkest thou thereof, Friar John?"

"Right well of you," said Friar John; "I find no Fault therein, save methinks that, as was formerly the Custom in War on the Day of Battle or Assault on a strong Place to promise the Soldiers double Pay for that Day—if they gained the Battle there would be Plenty to pay them with; if they lost, it would have been shameful to ask for it,[3] as the runaway Gruyers did after the Battle of Serizolles[4]— so likewise you ought to have reserved your Payment till the End, and the Money would have remained with you."

"'Twas well cacked for my Money," said Panurge." By

---

1 Rabelais in his journeys to and from Rome and Turin would go over Mont Cenis where tombs were to be seen in memory of travellers who had been lost in the snow.

2 *Land of Satin,* i.e. some unreal country represented only on tapestry like the story of Jonah and the whale. The land of Satin is described in v. 30, 31.

3 Erasm. *Apoph.* lib. V. (*Cato.* 24). Dixit Romanos errare [quod nollent accipere a Celtiberis sup-

petias ducenta talenta rogantibus] eo quod si vicissent reddituri fuerint, non de suo sed de bonis hostium: sin victi fuissent, jam non fore a quibus peteretur nec qui peterent. Plutarch, *Cato. Major* c. 10, 341 F.

4 *Gruyers.* The Swiss mercenaries at Ceresolles in Piedmont, under the Duc d'Enghien, April 11, 1544, ran away without a blow. The Imperialists under the Marquis de Guast were defeated. Brantome, I. 8 § 23.

the Powers, I have had Sport worth more than fifty thousand Francs.   Let us be gone now; the Wind is fair.

"Friar John, listen here.   Never did man do me a Good turn without a Recompense or at least an Acknowledgment.   I am not ungrateful, never was and never will be. Never did man do me an Ill turn without repenting it, either in this World or in the other.[1]   I am not such a Fool as that."

---

1 This sentiment seems to be derived from Pope Innocent, *de cont. mund.* iii. 15. "Ipse est judex justus qui nullum malum praeterit impunitum, nullum bonum inremuneratum." Cf. Jean Nevizan *Silv Nupt.* iv. § 124, Piers Plowman, C. v. 140, and Skeat's note.

# CHAPTER IV

How Pantagruel arrived at the Island of Ennasin,[1] and of the strange Relationships in that Land.

Zephyrus continued blowing for us in conjunction with a little of the Wind called Garbin,[2] and we had a Day pass without discovering Land.

On the third Day at the Flies' Dawn[3] there came in Sight a triangular Island bearing a very strong resemblance to Sicily in Form and Situation ; it was called the Island of Alliances.

The Men and Women are like the red-faced Poitevins, except that they all, Men, Women and little Children alike, have their Nose in the Shape of an Ace of Clubs ; for this reason the ancient Name of the Island was Ennasin ; and all the People were kindred and related together, as they boasted ; and the Magistrate of the Place told us frankly :

" You People of the other World hold it as an admirable Thing that[a] from one Roman Family (it was the Fabii) on one Day (it was the thirteenth of the Month of February)

a Ov. *Fasti*, ii. 105-242.

---

1 This chapter seems intended to satirize the forced puns, rebuses and common proverbs which do duty for conversation among certain "ennased" or noseless (*i.e.*, silly, senseless people.) It carries on the idea started in *Garg.* 9, and may be compared with Swift's " Polite Conversation."

2 *Garbino* in Italian and Spanish = S.W. wind ; in conjunction with Zephyrus it would make WSW.

3 *The Flies' Dawn*, the beginning of the afternoon when the flies are busy.

3

from one Gate (it was the *Porta Carmentalis,* since called
the *Porta Scelerata*) there went forth against certain
Enemies of the Romans (they were the Venetians)[1] three
hundred and six Men of War, all related.

Now from this Land of ours, in case of Need, more than
three hundred thousand could march forth, all Relations
and of one Family."

Their Kinships and Alliances were of a Fashion very
strange; for being thus all Relations and allied to one
another, we found that no one of them was Father or
Mother, Brother or Sister, Uncle or Aunt, Cousin or
Nephew, Son-in-law or Daughter-in-law, God-father or God-
mother, to any other, except indeed a tall noseless Old
man, who, as I saw, called a little Girl three or four years
old *Father,* while the little Girl called him *Daughter.*

The Relationship and Alliance between them was such
that one Man called a Woman my *Stock-fish ;* the Woman
called him my *Porpoise.*

"Those two," said Friar John, "ought to feel their Tide
well, when they rub their Bacon together."

One called another, my *Mattress ;* she called him, my
*Coverlet.*   Indeed he had some Marks of a Colin Clout
(rough Blanket).

One called another my *Crumb ;* she called him, my
*Crust.*

One called another his *Shovel ;* she called him her *Poker.*

One called another his *Shoe ;* she called him her *Slipper.*

One named another my *Boot ;* she called him her
*Sandal.*

---

1 *Venetians.* This mistake of A    *Veientes Hetrusques,* people of
is corrected in B, which reads    Veii in Etruria.

One named another his *Mitten;* she named him, my *Glove;* the Mitten has just brought in the Boot.

One named another his *Rind;* she called him her *Bacon,* and between them was begotten a Hog's leaf.

In like Kinship one called his Mate, *Omelette;* she named him my *Egg,* and they were akin, like an Omelette of Eggs.

In the same way another called his Lady-love, my *Tripe;* she called him her *Faggot,* and as yet I can never discover what Kindred, Alliance, Affinity or Consanguinity there was between them, with reference to our ordinary Usage, except that they told us that she was a Tripe of this Faggot.[1]

Another saluting a Friend of his, said: "Your Health my *Shell";* she answered: "The same to you my *Oyster."*

"That," said Carpalim, "is an [a]Oyster in a Shell."    a iv. 25, 32, 55.

Another in the same way saluted a Friend of his thus: "Good Life to you, my *Pod";* she answered: "A long one to you, sweet *Pea."*

"That," said Gymnast, "is a Pea in a Pod."

Another called his Friend, my *Sow;* she called him her *Hay.* Thereupon it came into my Thoughts that this Sow willingly turned to this Hay.[2]

I saw a little hunch-backed Gallant some little distance from us salute a Relation of his, saying: "Adieu, my *Hole";* she in the same style returned the Salute: "Heaven guard you, my *Peg!"*

Friar John said: "I believe she is all Hole and he like-

1 Fr. *tripe de fagot.* The meaning is uncertain. An explanation has been given that *tripe* is the smallest stick in a faggot.
2 From *tourner la truye au foin*

= to speak beside the question (*Garg.* 11). "Il corne à gauche. De *alliis* loquenti de *coepis* mihi respondet." Mat. Cordier *de corrupt. serm. emend.* 51, 12.

3—2

wise all Peg ; now it is a Question to know whether this
Hole can be totally stopped by that Peg."

Another saluted his Friend with the Words : " Good-bye
my *Coop*"; she answered: " Good-day my *Gosling.*"

" I believe," said Ponocrates, "that this Gosling is often
in the Coop."

A Groom talking with a young frisky Wench, said to
her : " Remember, *Fizzle.*" " I will not fail $F—t$,"
answered she.

Pantagruel said to the Magistrate : " Do you call those
two Relations ?   I think they must be Enemies, and not
akin to each other ; for he called her *Fizzle.*  In our
Country you could not insult a Woman more than by so
styling her."

" Good People of the other World," answered the
Magistrate, " you have few such Relations and so near as
are F—t and Fizzle here ; they proceeded invisibly both
together out of one Hole in an Instant."

" Then the Wind of Galerne,"[1] said Panurge, " had
lanternized their Mother."

" What Mother do you mean ? " said the Magistrate ;
" that is a Relationship of *your* World ; these have neither
Father nor Mother.   *That* is for People on the other side
of the Water, for Folk booted with Wisps of Hay."[2]

The good Pantagruel saw and heard all ; but at this
Talk he was well-nigh put out of countenance.

After having very carefully considered the Situation of
the Island, and the Manners of the *Ennased* People, we
went into a Tavern to refresh ourselves somewhat.   There

a Virg. *Georg.*,
iii., 273.

---

1 *Galerne* = N.W.          2 Fr. *bottés de foin, i.e.,* rough
                                uncultivated folk.

they were keeping a Wedding after the manner of the
Country ; bating that, there was rare good Cheer.

While we were there, a jovial Marriage was made between
a *Pear*, a Woman who was pretty gamesome, as we thought,
(however, those who had tasted her said she was flabby)
and a young *Cheese* with downy Hair, a little reddish.  I
had formerly heard the Talk about it, and elsewhere several
such Marriages had taken place ; they still say in our
[b]Cow-country that never was such a Marriage as is that [a] Pant.*Pr.*iv. 18.
between the Pear and the Cheese.[1]

In another Room I saw them marrying an old *Boot* to a
young, supple *Buskin*, and Pantagruel was told that the ,
young Buskin took the old Boot to Wife because she was
a comely Dame, fat and well-liking, and a Credit to her
House-keeping, were it even for a Fisherman.[2]

In another lower Room I saw a young *Pump* marry an
old *Slipper*, and we were told it was not for her Beauty or
good Grace, but from Avarice and Covetousness, to get
hold of the Crowns with which she was quilted.

1 Fr. *entre la poire et le fromage*,
a proverbial expression = at des
sert, when wine is drunk merrily.
2 *For a Fisherman.* There

seems to be a double allusion (1)
to a great fat housewife ; (2) to the
huge boots required by a fisherman.

# CHAPTER V

The South-west (*Garbin*) was blowing astern for us when,
leaving these unpleasant Alliancers[1] with their Ace-of-Club
Snouts, we put out into the open Sea.

About sundown we disembarked at the Island of Cheli,[2]
which was extensive, fertile, rich and populous; over it
reigned the good King Panigon,[3] who, accompanied by his
Children and the Princes of his Court, had come close down
to the Harbour to receive Pantagruel; and he led him to
his Castle.

At the Gate of the Donjon-Keep the Queen presented
herself accompanied by her Daughters and the Ladies of
her Court. Panigon desired her and all her Suite to kiss
Pantagruel and his Men. Such was the courteous Custom
of the Country.[4] This was done in every case except Friar
John, who absented himself and stood apart among the

---

1. Fr. *Allianciers* (sc. *de mots*)
*i.e.*, persons guilty of *mauvaises
plaisanteries*.

2 *Cheli* probably derived from
χεῖλη, lips, lip-courtesy, com-
pliments, &c.

3 *Panigon* has been explained
as πᾶν εἴκων, "easy-yielding."

4 This is noted by Erasmus as
the custom in England: Sunt hic
nymphae divinis vultibus, blandae,
faciles, et mos numquam satis
laudatus; quo venias omnium
osculis excipieris, sive discedas
osculis dimitteris, redis redduntur
suavia, disceditur dividuntur basia;
quocumque te moveas suaviorum
sunt omnia plena.

King's Officers.   Panigon tried by every possible Entreaty
to keep Pantagruel with him for this Day and the next.
Pantagruel founded his Excuse on the Calmness of the
Weather and the Favourableness of the Wind, which is
more often wished for than met with by Travellers, and the
Necessity of using it when it comes, for it does not come
always, nor as often as one wishes for it.[1]

On this Plea, after we had drunk five-and-twenty or
thirty times each, Panigon let us go.

Pantagruel, returning to the Port and not seeing Friar
John, asked whereabouts he was and why he was not with
the Company.   Panurge knew not how to excuse him, and
wanted to return to the Castle to summon him, when Friar
John ran up quite joyous and cried out in mighty Gaiety of
Heart, saying :

"Long live the noble Panigon !   By the Death of the
wooden Ox, he[a] revels in the Kitchen.   That is where I    *Garg.*, II.
come from ; everything there goes by Bucketfuls.   I was in
good Hopes to have stuffed the Mould of my Frock[2] for
my Use and Profit as a Monk should."

"So, my Friend," said Pantagruel ; "always in these
Kitchens ? "

"Pullet's Body," answered Friar John, "I know the
Customs and Ceremonies there better than to fiddle-faddle
with these Women.   *Magny, magna, fiddle-faddle,* Cringes,
double Honours, the Embrace, *beso las manos de vuestra
Merced,* of your Majesty, of your Excellence, be most

[1] Talia sunt ut optata magis
quam inventa videantur.   Cic.
*N. Deor.* i. § 19.

[2] *The Mould of my Frock,* i.e.,
stomach.   So the head is called

*moule de bonnet* in *Garg.* 9.   Le
molle de noz chapperons.   *Moralité
d'ung empereur.*   (Ancien Théâtre
Français, iii. p. 144).

welcome, [b] *Tarabin, tarabas.* Rot! that is 'Muck' at Rouen, with all this cringing and faddling about! Bah! I do not say that I do not sometimes take a Pull above the Dregs in my homely Fashion, so as to allow me to put in my Nomination;[1] but this Rubbish of bowing and scraping vexes me more than a young Devil—I meant to say a double Fast.[2] In that St. Benedict never lied."[3]

By the Powers, why do we not betake our Humanities into some fair Kitchen of God, and there contemplate the Rattling and Harmony of the Spits, the Temperature of the Soups, the Preparations for the Dessert, the Order of the Wine-service?[4] *Beati immaculati in via.* 'Tis in the Breviary."[5]

"That," said Epistemon, "is spoken like a true Monk; I say like a monking Monk, I do not say a bemonked Monk. Indeed you bring back to my Recollection what I saw and heard in Florence twelve years ago.[6]

"We were a goodly Company of Studious folk eager to see the Antiquities and Curiosities of Italy; and at that time we were carefully considering the Situation and

1 Cf. *Arrêt d'Amours,* No. 52. De l'heure que l'homme est marié il ne luy est loisible de faire l'amoureux *n'insinuer sa nomination* sur une autre que sa femme . . . pour ce que pluralité de tels bénéfices est reprouvée de droit naturel et positif d'amours. Cf. *Garg.* 5.

2 An untranslatable pun on *Jeune Diable* and *Jeûne double.*

3 Brother John, as a Benedictine, must needs maintain his patron's veracity. He here limits it to the point concerning the double fast.

4 Fr. *l'ordre du service du vin* for *service divin* as in *Garg.* 27. Cf. also v. 46, *l'homme de vin divin devient.*

5 *Breviary.* Ps. cxviii. is sung on Fridays, and other times at Prime.

6 *Twelve years ago.* This would refer to Rabelais' journey *to* Rome in 1535, supposing this to have been written in 1547. It could scarcely have taken place in the hurried departure *from* Rome in 1536. B (published in 1552) substitutes "about *twenty* years."

Beauty of Florence, the Structure of the Duomo, the Sumptousness of the Temples and magnificent Palaces, and striving to outdo one another as to which should most fittingly extol them with Praises according to their Merits, when a Monk of Amiens, named Bernard Lardon, as though quite vexed, said to us :

"'I don't know what the Deuce you find so much to praise here. I have had my Eyes about me as well as you, and I am not blind any more than you are. Now after all what is it? These be fine Houses; that's all. But God and my Master Saint Bernard, our good Patron, be with us! In the whole of this City as yet I have not seen a single Cook-shop.

"Now in Amiens in four times less walking than we have had in our Contemplations I could shew you more than fourteen Cook-shops. I don't know what Pleasure you have taken in seeing the Lions and Africans[1]—so methinks you styled, or perhaps it was Libystian Bears, what people call Tigers—near the Belfry,[2] likewise in seeing the Porcupines and Ostriches in the Palace of the Lord Philip Storzy.[3] By my Faith, my Sons, I would like better to see a good fat Gosling on a Spit.

"This Porphyry and these Marbles are fine; I say nothing against them; but the Tartlets of Amiens are

---

1 Servius on *Aen.* v. 37, *pelle Libystidis ursae* raises a doubt whether it was the skin, " re vera *ursae,* aut ferae Africanae, id est leonis aut .pardi." Tigers are called *Africanae* by Cicero, Livy and Pliny.

2 The Belfry refers to the high slender tower on the *Palazzo*

*Vecchio,* at the north corner of which there is a marble lion.

3 Filippo Strozzi, a rich Florentine merchant, who had married Clarice, the aunt of Catharine de' Medici, and was father of Pierre Strozzi, the French marshal. His magnificent palace built by Cronaca still exists.

better.  These ancient Statues are beautifully made, I am willing to believe it ; but by Saint Ferreol[1] of Abbeville the young Wenches of our Country are a thousand times more attractive ? ' "

"What doth it signify and what is the Meaning," asked Friar John, "that in Kitchens you always find Monks, never do you find Kings, Popes or Emperors.  Is there some latent Virtue and specific Property hidden in the Kettles and Racks, which attracts Monks thither, as the Loadstone draweth to itself the Iron,[2] but doth not attract Popes, Emperors or Kings ; or is it a natural Inclination attaching to Frocks, which of itself leads and impels those good Religious men into the Kitchen, even though they had not elected or resolved to go thither ? "

"It means," auswered Epistemon, "Forms following Matter ; so doth Averroës call them."[3]

"Yea verily, verily,"[4] quoth Friar John.

"I will tell you," answered Pantagruel, "without giving an Answer to the Problem set before us.  For it is somewhat ticklish, and you can hardly handle it without pricking yourself.  I remember to have read that [a]Antigonus, King of Macedonia, going one day into the Kitchen of his Tents and there coming upon the Poet Antagoras, who was frying Congers and himself holding the Pan, asked him : 'Was Homer frying Congers when he was describing the Prowess of Agamemnon ? ' "

a Plut. *Apoph.* c. 17. 182 F.

1 *Ferreol.*  " Les uns disent que saint Feriol est le plus habile à garder les oyes." (H. Estienne, *Apol. p. Hérod.* c. xxxviii.)

2 Comme la pierre de l'aiment, Trait à soi le fer soutilment.    ℞ 1165.

3 In primo physicae (Aristotelis)

dictum est quod femina appetit virum et turpe appetit bonum, sicut materia appetit formam. (Transl. of Th. Gaza). Cf. *Phys.* i. 9, 192a, 16-26.

4 Fr. *voire, voire.* Cf. "vero, vero," inquit Habinnas. Petron. c. 72.

" Antagoras answered : ' O King, thinkest thou that Agamemnon when he was performing his mighty Deeds was curious to know if anyone in his Camp was frying Congers?'

" The King found it ill that Poets should be found in his Kitchen ; the Poet pointed out to him that it was a Matter far more indecent to meet with Kings there."

With this Gossip they came down to their Ships and made no longer Stay in the Island of Cheli.

# CHAPTER VI

How Pantagruel passed Procuration and of the
Strange Manner of living among the Catchpoles.

FILLED and crammed with the good Treatment of King
Panigon we continued our Course. The following Day we
passed Procuration,[1] which is a Country all blotted.[2] I
could make nothing of it.

There we saw Pettifoggers[3] and Catchpoles, Folk with
their Hair on.[4] They invited us neither to eat nor drink,
they only told us that they were at our Service—if we paid
them.

One of our Interpreters related to Pantagruel how this
People gained their Living in a Fashion very strange and
diametrically opposite to that of the Dwellers in Rome.[5]
At Rome an infinite Number of people gain their Liveli-
hood by poisoning, killing and beating; the Catchpoles
gain theirs by being beaten, so that if they were long with-

1 *Passed Procuration* has two
meanings, (1) passed by the Island
Procuration, and (2) passed through
the Court by means of Attorneys.
Cf. *Pant.* 17.

2 *Blotted* with the erasures and
ink of the Pettifogers.

3 Fr. *Procultoux*, should properly be *procureurs*, which in
common parlance became *pro-
culous*. It is here changed into

*procultoux*, "tramplers on all."
*Procultour* occurs in Chaucer *Frere's
Tale*, D. 1596 cf. Skeat, vol. v.
p. 329.

4 Fr. *à tout* (= *avec*) *le poil* (cf.
*Pant.* 2 *fin*) folks who will stick at
nothing.

5 Fr. *Romicoles*, i.e., the spa-
dassins and assassins. See the Life
of Benvenuto Cellini *passim*.

out being beaten they would die of downright Starvation,
they, their Wives and their Children.[1]

"This," said Panurge, "is like those who according to
the Relation of Cl. Galen cannot erect their cavernous
Nerve[a] towards the Equatorial Circle if they be not  [a] *Pant.* 26.
thoroughly well whipped. By St. Thibaut,[2] whoso should
whip me would make me quite contrariwise dismount, in
the Name of all the Devils."

"The Method," said the Pilot, "is in this way : When
a Priest, a Usurer, or an Advocate wishes ill to some Gentleman of his Country he sends to him one of these Catchpoles. Catchpole will summon him, serve a Writ on him,
abuse him and affront him impudently in pursuance of his
Record and Instruction, insomuch that the Gentleman, if
he be not paralysed in his Senses and more stupid than a
gyrine[b] Frog (Tadpole), will be constrained to give him  [b] Plat. *Theaet.*
Bastinadoes and Sword-strokes on the Head, or to have  161 D. Erasm. *Ad.* ii. i. 34.
him thrown from the Battlements or Windows of his Castle.

"This done, you have your Catchpole rich for four
Months, as though Blows from a Stick were his real
Harvest. For he will have a thoroughly good Salary from
the Priest or the Advocate, and Reparation from the
Gentleman, sometimes so great that the Gentleman will
thereby lose all that he has, besides being in danger of
rotting in Prison miserably, as though he had struck the
King."

"I remember," said Pantagruel, "on this Subject a [c]Story  [c] Gell. xx. 1 § 13.
of a Roman Gentleman named L. Neratius. He was of a

---

1 Frappez, j'ai quatre enfants à
      nourrir,
  L'Intime in *Les Plaideurs*, ii. 4.
Racine has caught his inspiration
from this chapter.

2 St. Thibaut of Champagne in
the 11th century was a great fla-
gellant.

noble Family and rich in his time; but he had such a
tyrannical Complexion that as he set forth from his Palace,
he caused the Purse and Pouch of his Servants to be
filled with gold and silver Coin; and as he met in the
Streets some conceited Dandies who were better dressed
than ordinary, without Provocation from them, in mere
Wantonness he would give them heavy Blows in the Face
with his Fist. Immediately after, to appease them and
prevent them from laying a Plaint in a Court of Justice, he
would give them of his Money as a Sauce to his Fisticuffs,
so that he made them contented and satisfied according to
the Ordinance of a Law of the Twelve Tables.[1] Thus he
expended his Revenue, beating the People for the Price of
his Money."

Friar John of the Trencherites said : "By the holy Boot
of St. Benêt[2] I will know the Truth of it at once."

Accordingly he put his Hand to his Fob and drew out
ten Sun-crowns; then he said in a loud Voice in the
hearing of a large Crowd of the Catchpole people: "Who
wishes to earn ten Sun-crowns for being beaten like the
Devil?"

"Io, Io, Io,"[3] they all answered; and they ran up in a
Crowd to see who should be first in date to be beaten at so
good a Price.

Friar John chose out of the whole Troop a Catchpole
with a red Muzzle, who wore on the Thumb of his Right
hand a thick broad Silver Ring.

---

1 The Law of the XII. Tables
ran thus: SI INIVRIAM ALTERI
FAXSIT VIGINTI QVINQVE AERIS
POENAE SVNTO.

2 The holy Boot (*Botta*) of St.

Benêt was a large tun of the
Benedictines at Bologna. Cf.
*Garg.* 39, and v. 47. For the pun,
cf. iv. 43.

3 *Io*, Italian for " I."

When he had picked him out I saw that all the People murmured ; it was from Jealousy, and I heard a tall, young Catchpole, who was a skilful and good Scholar and, as common Report went, an honest Man in the Ecclesiastical Court, complaining and saying that Red-muzzle took from them all their Practice, and that if there were only thirty Blows of a Cudgel to earn in all the Land he always pocketed eight-and-twenty and a half of them.[1]

Friar John belaboured him so much, Back and Belly, Arms and Legs, Head and all, with mighty Blows from his Cudgel, that I took him to be beaten to death ; then he gave him the ten Crowns, and behold the Rascal was on his Legs as pleased as a Couple of Kings. The others said to Friar John : "Sir, Sir, Brother Devil, if it please you again to beat some of us, we are all at your Service." They made the same Offer to Panurge and to Gymnast and others ; but no one would listen to them.

Afterwards, as we were seeking fresh Water for the Ships' Crews, we found two old She-catchpoles of the Place, who were miserably weeping and lamenting together. Pantagruel, suspecting they were related to the Catchpole who had received the Bastinado, asked them the Reasons for such Grief.

They replied that they had a very good Reason for weeping, seeing that at that very Hour two of the honestest

---

1 L'INTIME.
　　Et si dans la province
Il se donnoit en tout vingt coups
　　de nerf de bœuf,

Mon père, pour sa part, en em-,
　　boursoit dix-neuf.
　　Racine, *Les Plaideurs*, i. 5.

People in all Catchpole-land had been led to the Gibbet to be hanged.

When they were questioned as to the Reasons for this Hanging they answered that they had stolen the Instruments of the Mass.[1]

1 The " tradition (or porrection) of the Instruments," or giving of the paten and the chalice to the newly ordained, now forms part of the essentials of western ordination. St. Thomas affirms it to belong to the form of the sacrament. (*Xn. and Eccl. Rome*, pt. ii., p. 172).

# CHAPTER VII

## How Pantagruel passed the Islands of Tohu and Bohu, and of the strange Death of Nose-slitter the Swallower of Windmills

THAT same day Pantagruel passed the two Islands of Tohu and Bohu[1] in which we found nothing to fry.[2]

Nose-slitter,[3] the great Giant, in default of Windmills which were his ordinary Diet, had swallowed up all the Pots and Pans, Kettles, Skillets and Saucepans in the Country. Whence it had come about that a little before Daybreak, about the Hour of his Digestion, he had fallen ill of a grievous Malady, from a certain Crudity of Stomach caused, as the Physicians of the Place said, by the Fact that the concocting Faculty of his Stomach, naturally disposed to digest Mills, had not been able perfectly to digest the Pots and Skillets; the Kettles and Saucepans he had pretty well digested, as they said they knew by the Sediments and Eneoremes[4] of three Tuns of Urine which he had passed that Morning.

---

1 *Tohu and Bohu* are two Hebrew words signifying "solitude" and "void." Cf. Genesis, i. 2. Et erat terra solitudo (*tohu*) et inanitas (*bohu*). Vulg.

2 *Il n'a que frire* Nullam habet rem familiarem. Cordier, 58, 17.

3 Fr. *Bringuenarilles = fendeur de nez*, from German *brechen*. (Le Duchat). Cf. Hom. *Od.* xviii. 84.
πέμψω σ᾽ ἠπειρόνδε βαλὼν
ἐν νηΐ μελαίνῃ,

εἰς Ἔχετον βασιλῆα βροτῶν
δηλήμονα πάντων,
ὅς κ᾽ ἀπὸ ῥῖνα τάμῃσι καὶ
οὔατα νηλέϊ χαλκῷ.
Some of the notions in this chapter, and iv. 44, are borrowed from *Le Disciple de Pantagruel*, cc. iv-ix.

4 De *hypostasi* urinae et ejus significationibus . . . supernatat *eneorema*. Averroes *Colliget*, iv. 24. Hippocr. *Epid.* i. 2 (p. 983, Kühn).

4

To relieve him they employed divers Remedies in accordance with their Art. But the Disease was stronger than the Remedies, and the noble Nose-slitter had died that Morning in a Manner so strange that you should no longer wonder at the Death of Aeschylus.—It had been told him, in accordance with the Fates, that on a certain Day he should die by the Coming-down of something that should fall upon him. On that predestined Day he had removed himself from all Houses, Trees, Rocks and other Things which could fall and by their Falling hurt him; and he remained in a great Meadow, trusting himself to the Faith of the free and open Sky in well-assured Security, as he thought; unless indeed the Sky should fall, which he believed to be impossible.

Nevertheless it is said that the Larks dread it;[1] for if the Sky should fall they would all be taken. So also formerly did the Gymnosophists of India fear this,[2] who when asked by Alexander the Great what it was they feared most in this World, answered that they feared nothing save the Sky falling.

[a] Val. Max. ix. 12, 8.     Notwithstanding all this,[a] Aeschylus died by the Coming-down and Fall of a Tortoise-shell which, falling on his Head from the Claws of an Eagle high in Air, dashed out his Brains.——

[b] V.M. ix., 12, E. 8.     Nor need you wonder at the Death of Anacreon the Poet[b] who died choked by a Grape-stone;

---

[1] *Larks dread the sky falling.* This is a proverb found in other languages (cf. *Garg.* 11.) Instances in our old dramatists. Cf. Dodsley's *Old Plays*, ix. p. 166, xii. p. 353.

[2] In B this is attributed to the Celts living near the Rhine, that is the French, in a passage translated from Arrian *Anab.* i. 4, 7-8.

Nor at that of ᶜFabius the Roman Praetor, who was ᶜ Plin. vii. 7, §5.
choked by a Goat's Hair, as he was eating a Bowl of Milk ;
Nor at that of the ᵈbashful Man who, in default of letting ᵈ Suet. v. 32.
go an unpleasant Odour, died in the Presence of the
Emperor Claudius ;
Nor at that of him who is buried near the Flaminian.
Gate at Rome, who in his Epitaph[1] complains that his
Death was caused by the Bite of a Cat on his little Finger ;
Nor at that of Guignemauld, a Norman Physician, a great
Swallower of grey Peas and a very distinguished Gambler,
who died suddenly from not having paid his Debts, and
from having taken a Worm out of his Hand side-ways with
a Pen-knife ;
Nor at that of Spurius Saufeius who died supping a soft-
boiled Egg as he came out of the Bath ;[2]
Nor of any others you are told of, whether by Verrius,
or Pliny, or Valerius, or Baptista Fulgosus or Bacabery the
elder or ᵉMaul-Chitterling.                                    e Cf. iv. 37.
The good Nose-slitter died (alas !) choked through eating
a Lump of fresh Butter at the Mouth of a hot Oven by the
Order of his Physicians.
Moreover we were told that the King of Cullan[3] in Bohu
had defeated the Satraps of King Mechloth[4] and sacked the
Fortresses of Belima.[5]

1 *Epitaph.* It is on the floor on
the left side of the nave, in the
Church of S. Maria del Popolo
(sometimes called in documents of
Saec. xv. S.M. ad Flaminiam) just
inside the gate on the *via Flaminia*;
Hospes, disce novum mortis genus ;
    improba felis,
Dum trahitur, digitum mordet et
    intereo.
2 Non major ea res fuit nec
minus nova qua Spurius (Appius.

Plin. vii. § 54). Saufeius interiit cum
balneum egressus ovum sorberet.
    Baptista Fulgosus, *de inusitatis
        mortis generibus,* ix. c. 12.
    3 *Cullan* is unknown, possibly
intended for Cologne.
    4 *Mechloth* probably metathesis
of the Hebrew *meloheth* ▬ king-
dom. Cf. *malachoth.* Dante *Par.*
vii. 3.
    5 *Belima* (Heb.) = nothing.

# CHAPTER VIII.

## How Pantagruel encountered a Great Storm at Sea.

THE next Day we passed to starboard of a Craft laden with Monks,

a iii. 22.

a Cordeliers,

a Jacobins,

b iii. 23.

b Carmelites,

Augustinians,[1]

Celestins,[2]

a Capuchins,

Bernardins,[3]

a Minims,

c *Pant.* 7.

c Jesuits,

Benedictines[4]

and other holy Religious men who were going to the Council of Chesil[5] to discuss the Articles of the Faith against the new Heretics.

On seeing them Panurge fell into an Excess of Delight, and having courteously saluted the blessed Fathers and recommended the Salvation of his Soul to their devout

---

1 Alexander IV. in 1256 united all the Hermits under one order, and subjected them to the rule of St. Augustine; hence they were known as the *Hermits of St. Augustine*, and formed one of the four Mendicant orders.

2 *Celestins* were a separate order of Benedictines, founded in 1294 by Pietro di Morone afterwards Pope Celestine V. Cf. *Pant.* 7.

3 *Bernardins*, founded by St. Bernard of Clairvaux.

4 In 510 St. Benedict accepted the rule over the monks of Vico Varo as their Abbot, and founded the Benedictine order.

5 *Chesil* was for the Hebrews the star of storm, as Orion for the Greeks. The Council of Chesil means the Council of Trent, which sat from 1547 to 1563, with several interruptions.

Prayers and private Orisons, he caused to be thrown on board their Ship sixteen Dozens of Hams, and two thousand fine Angels[1] for the Souls of the Departed.

Pantagruel remained quite pensive and melancholy. Friar John perceived it and was asking him whence proceeded such unusual Sadness, when the Pilot, observing the Fluttering of the Pennant above the Poop catch an ugly Squall and a fresh Hurricane, had all Hands piped on Deck, Officers, Sailors and Ship-boys, as well as Passengers ; had the Sails taken down, Mizzen-sail, Mizzen-topsail, Lug-sail, Main-sail, Pulleys, Sprit-sail ; had the Top-sails hauled down, Fore-top and Main-top ; lowered the Mizzen-mainsail and all the Yard-arms, leaving only the Rattlings and the Shrouds.[2]

Suddenly the Sea began to swell and rage from its lowest Depths,[3]

The mighty Waves to beat on our Ship's Sides,

The Mistral with a furious Hurricane, black Squalls, terrible Whirlwinds, deadly Gusts to whistle through our Yards ;

The Heaven thundered from above ; there were Thunderings,[4] Lightnings, Rain, Hail ;

1 *Angels.* (Fr. *Angelotz*) gold pieces dating from Charles VI. of France, minted in great numbers in the reigns of Henry V. and Henry VI. of England, worth about 10 shillings, and bearing the figure of St. Michael.

2 Vidit et ascortus jam plurima
  signa paronus,
  Ex quibus agnovit quod magna
  procella minezzat.
  .    .    .    .    .
  Quid facit? appocum sua vela
  magister abassat,

Denudat brazzos, plantans se
  retro timoni,
Plurima sollicitis famulis gridando comandat,
Cui parent omnes facientes
  mille facendas,
Hic molat cordam, tirat ipse,
  revinculat alter.
    Merl. Coc. xi. 363-4, 374-8.

3 Audivere maris sub fundamenta moveri.—M. C. xi. 369.

4 Pro quibus astra tonant, tremit orbis, nutat olympus.—M. C. xii. 11.

The Air lost its Brightness and grew thick, dark and overcast, so that no other Light shewed to us than that of the Thunderbolts, Flashes of Lightning and Rendings of the blazing Clouds.[1]

The Hurricanoes, Flaws, Squalls and Whirlwinds lighted up all around us with Thunder-bolts, Flashes and Forked Lightning and other aërial Jaculations;[2]

Our Looks were full of Amazement and Dismay, while the awful Tornadoes hung in the Clouds the mountainous Billows of the Ocean.[3]

Believe me, we thought it was the Return of the ancient Chaos, in which Fire, Air, Sea, Land, all the Elements were in refractory Confusion.

Panurge, having with the Contents of his Stomach plentifully fed the scatophagous Fish, was all of a heap on the Deck, utterly cast down; utterly matagrabolised and half dead as he was, he invoked the twin Sons of Leda and the Egg-shell from which they were hatched,[4] and roared out in terrible Fright :

1 Non plus bianca diem spar-
    pagnat luna per orbem,
  Nubila tetra volant ventis
    agitata nefandis;
  Fulgure flammigero tantum
    lampezat Olympus.
          M.C. xii. 18-20.

2 Fr. Les *categides, thielles, le-
lapes* et *presteres* enflamber tout
autour de nous par les *psoloentes,
arges, elicies* et autres ejaculations
etherées. The Greek words here
used are to be found in this exact
order in (Aristot.) *de Mundo,* c. 4,
of which there is a Latin translation
by Budaeus.

3 Fr. *typhones.* Scandebatque
altum girans aëronus Olympum,
M.C., xii. Sed nihil de periculo
neque de saevitia venti remissum
quin turbines etiam crebriores et
caelum atrum et fumigantes globi
et figurae quaedam nubium metu-
endae, quos "*typhonas*" vocabant
impendere imminereque ac depres-
surae navem videbantur. Gell.
xix. 1 § 3.

4 Cingar solettus cantone jace-
    bat in uno,
  Qui metuendo mori cagarolam
    tristis habebat,

  .      .      .      .

  Omnibus o quales sanctis facit
    ille prigheras ! — M.C. xii.
  83-4, 90.
Of the eggs laid by Leda it is said
in the *Hypnerotomachia,* c. 14.
De l'un de ces œufs sortait une
flamme, de l'autre deux belles
etoiles: VNI . GRATVM . MARE .
ALTERVM . GRATVM . MARI.
    Popelin's Trans. vol. i. p 270.

" What ho! Steward, my Friend, my Father, my Uncle,
bring me a little Salt pork.   We shall have only too much
to drink soon, from what I see.   *Eat little and drink more*
will be my Motto hereafter.   Would to God I could be on
*Terra firma* and well at mine Ease.

" O three and four times [d]happy are those who plant     d Verg. *A.* i. 94.
Cabbages!

" O Fates, why did you not spin me for a Planter of
Cabbages!

" O [e]small is the Number of those to whom Jupiter hath     e Id. *A.* vi. 129.
shewn such Favour that he has destined them to plant
Cabbages!   Happy folk! for they have always one Foot
on land and the other is not far from it."[1]

Let whoso will dispute on Felicity and the *summum
bonum*, but whoever plants Cabbages is at once by my
Decree declared most fortunate; and with far better Reason
than [f]Pyrrho had, who, being in Danger like that in which     f Diog. L. ix. 11.
we are and seeing a Hog near the Shore eating Barley     68.
littered before him, declared him to be most happy in two
Respects, namely that he had Barley in plenty, and over
and above that, was on Land.   O for a deific and lordly
Habitation there is nothing like a [g]Cow's Floor.     g *Pant.* Prol. iv.
9.

This Wave will sweep us away, blessed Saviour!   O my
Friends, a little Vinegar; I sweat again with sheer Agony.
Iarus![2] the Halyards are broken, the Main-tackling is all to
pieces, the Sides are sprung, the Maintop-masthead plunges
into the Sea, the Keel is up to the Sky; our Shrouds are

---

1 *Not far from it*, i.e., on a spade.
2 *Jarus!* This exclamation of
distress is replaced in B throughout by *Zalos!*  It is probably a
German expression picked up at

Metz.   There is a German student-
song of which the refrain runs:
    O jerum, jarum, jerum!
    Qualis mutatio rerum!

nearly all burst.  Iarus!  Iarus!  where are our Top-sails?
All is *frelore bigoth!*[1]  Our Top-mast is run adrift.  Iarus!
into whose possession shall this Wreck come?[2]
Friends, help here behind one of these Bends.  My
Lads, your Stay-tackling is fallen.

Alas, do not let go the Tiller, or the Tackle; I hear the
Pintle crack.  Is it broken?

For Heaven's sake let us save the Rudder-stopper; don't
trouble yourselves about the Ring.

Bebebe, bous, bous, bous, Iarus!  Look at the Needle
of your Compass, I beseech you, Master Astrophil,[3] and
tell us whence this Hurricane comes.

---

1 *All is frelore* = Germ. *Alles ist
verloren bei Gott.*  This is the
refrain of a celebrated song by
Cl. Jannequin (reprinted Venice,
1550) on the defeat of the Swiss at
Marignano (Sept. 13, 1515).
  Tout est frelore,
  La tintelore,
  Tout est frelore bigot.

*Tout frelore* occurs also in Patelin
l. 742.
  2 *Into whose possession, &c.* alluding to the rights to wreckage
which formerly existed (Lacroix).
Cf. Martial vi. 62, 4:
  Cujus vulturis hoc erit cadaver?
  3 *Astrophil* (Gr.) = star - lover,
i.e., pilot.

# CHAPTER IX

## WHAT COUNTENANCES PANURGE AND FRIAR JOHN KEPT DURING THE STORM

PANTAGRUEL by the Pilot's Advice held the Mast tight and firm;[1] Friar John had stripped himself to his Doublet to help the Seamen; so had Epistemon, Ponocrates and the others.

Panurge remained squatting on the Deck, weeping and lamenting. Friar John perceived him, as he was going on the Quarter-deck, and said to him: Pardy! Panurge the Calf, Panurge the Weeper, Panurge the Wailer, thou wouldest do much better to help us here than to blubber away there like a Cow, squatted on thy Cods like a Baboon."

"Be, be, be, bous, bous, bous!" answered Panurge; "Friar John, my Friend, my good Father, I drown, I drown, my Friend, I am drowning. I am clean done for, my ghostly Father, my Friend, I am clean gone; your Cutlass could not save me from this.[2]

"Iarus! Iarus! we are above the *E la*, entirely above the Scale. Be, be, be, bous, bous! Iarus! now we are below the *Gamma ut*.[3] I am drowning!

1 Talia dum Cingar trepido sub
  pectore volvit

  .    .    .

  Baldus firma stetit veluti ve-
  chissima quercus.
          —M.C. xii. 97-101.

2 As it did from the Sheep-dealer at the end of c. 2.

3 *E la* is the highest, as *Ut* is the lowest in the old musical scale.

Nunc sbalzata ratis summum
  toccabat olympum,
Nunc subit infernam unda sba-
  dacchiante paludem.
        —M.C. xii. 10-11.
Deque *ci sol fa ut* modulando
  surgit ad *ela*.

  .    .    .

Pollicis exterius nodos trapassat
in *ut re*.
      M.C. xx. 155-167.

"Ah! my Father, my Uncle, my All, the Water has got into my Shoes by my Shirt-collar. Bous, bous, bous, paisch; hu, hu, hu, hu, ha, ha, ha! Hu, hu, hu, hu, hu, hu! Bebe, bous, bous, bobous, bobous, ho, ho, ho, ho, ho! Iarus, Iarus! Just now I am rarely playing the forked Tree, with my Feet in the Air and my Head below.

"Would to God I were at this moment in the Ship of those good and blessed Concilipetous Fathers whom we met this Morning, who were so godly, so fat, so merry, and so gracious!¹

"Holos, holos, holos! Iarus! this Wave of all the Devils —(*mea culpa, Deus*) I mean this Wave of God—will break up our Ship. Iarus! Friar John, my Father, my Friend, "Confession"! See me here on my Knees. *Confiteor;* your holy Blessing!"

"Come, thou devilish Hang-dog," said Friar John, come hither and help us; by thirty Legions of Devils come! Art coming?"

"Let us not swear at all at this time," said Panurge, "my Father, my Friend. To-morrow as much as you will."

"Holos, holos, Iarus! Our Ship lets Water, I drown. Iarus! Iarus! Be, be, be be be, bous, bous, bous, good People, bous! Now we are at the Bottom. Iarus! Iarus! I will give eighteen hundred thousand Crowns a year to the Man who will put me ashore, all bewrayed and bedaubed as I am, as much as any man ever was in my Country of Pickle. *Confiteor.* Iarus!"

"May a thousand Devils jump on the Body of this

1 Heu! cur non potius monachi vel norma severi,     Vel mage eremitæ placuit sacra cellula nobis?
     M.C. xii. 42-3.

Cuckold!" said Friar John. "By the Powers, art thou talking of Confession at this Time while we are in Danger, and while we ought to bestir ourselves, now or never? Ho, wilt thou come, Devil?

"Boatswain, my hearty! O the rare Lieutenant! This side, Gymnast, on the Poop.

"Boy there! by all the Devils mind the Pump. Hast hurt thyself? Zounds, fasten it to one of these Blocks; here, on that Side, i' the Devil's Name. Ha! so, my Boy."

"Ah! Friar John," said Panurge, "my ghostly Father, my Friend, let us not swear; you do sin. Iarus! Iarus! Bebebe, bous, bous! I drown, I am dying, my Friends. I am in Charity with all the World. Farewell! Iarus! *In manus!* Bous, bous bouououous!

"St. Michael of Aure![1] St. Nicholas![2] Help at this time, now or never! I make you here a solemn Vow, and to Our Lord, that if, as at this time, you are my Helpers—I mean that you put me ashore out of this Danger—I will build you a fine grand little Chapel or two

> Where 'twixt Quande and Monsoreau
> There shall feed nor Calf nor Cow.[3]

Iarus! Iarus! more than eighteen Bucketfuls or two have got into my Mouth. Bous, bous, bous! How salt and bitter it is!"

"By the Powers," said Friar John, "of the Blood, the Flesh, the Belly, the Head, if I hear thee again howling,

1 *St. Michael of Aure.* Possibly St. Michael *ad auras* cf. *Pant.* 17. Churches dedicated to this saint were often on high cliffs by the sea. He was specially St. Michael *au peril de la mer.*

2 *St. Nicholas* is the patron saint of sailors. *Legenda Aurea,* iii. 3.

3 Cande and Montsoreau (*Garg.* 47) are adjoining, and therefore nothing could feed *between* them.

thou devilish Cuckold, I will maul thee like any Sea-wolf. By the Powers why don't we throw him to the Bottom of the Sea?

"Jack, there, my honest Fellow; so my Lad, so. Hold fast there above.

"Verily there is a rare lot of Lightning and Thundering! I believe all the Devils have broken loose to-day, or that Proserpine is in Labour. All the Devils are dancing a Horn-pipe."

"Ah!" said Panurge, "you sin, Friar John, my former Friend. It goes against my Heart to tell you so; for I believe that it does you great Good to swear thus. Nevertheless you do sin my sweet Friend."

"A thousand," said Friar John, "nay, hundreds of millions of Devils, seize the hornified devilish Cuckold. Just help us here, Bougre, Lubber[1] of all the Devils, *incubi, succubi* and all that ever are. Come on here, on the Port side. 'Ods Head full of Relics![2] What Ape's Paternoster is it thou art muttering there between thy Teeth? This Devil of a Sea-calf is the Cause of the Storm, and he is the only one who does not help the Crew, and yet he worries us with his Cries. I swear, if I go thither, I will chastise you like any Sea Devil. Here, Mate, my Lad, hold this tight while I tie a Greek Knot. O the brave Boy! I would to God thou wert Abbot of Talemont,[3] and that he who is there now were Guardian of le Croullay![4]

---

1 Fr. *bredasse* ou *bredache* = étourdi, écervelé (Becherelle's Dictionary.) In B. *Tigre* is substituted for this violent sentence.

2 A favourite oath of the Seigneur de la Roche du Maine (*Briefve déclaration*).

3 *Talemont* is an abbey in Touraine. In B. *Talemouse* ( = cheese-cake), is substituted to furnish a pun on *mousse* = boy.

4 *Le Croullay*, near Chinon, where was a Franciscan convent.

" Brother Ponocrates, you will hurt yourself there.

"Epistemon, keep clear of the Hatchway; I saw a Thunder-bolt fall there just now.

" Haul away, up there !—

" Right you are " ——

" Haul, haul, haul !  Clear the Long-boat ; haul away !

" By the Powers, what is that?  The Ship's-head is knocked to pieces.  Hang that Wave.  I swear it almost swept me away into the Current.  I believe all the Devils are holding their Provincial Chapter here.          .

"Port there !"—Port it is, Sir.—" Mind your Noddle, Boy, in the Devil's name !  Port !  Port ! "

" Bebebebous, bous, bous," said Panurge, " bous, bous, bous, I am drowning.  I see neither Heaven nor Earth. Iarus !  Would that it had pleased the worthy Goodness of God that at this very hour I were within the ªClose at   ª *Garg.* 27. Seuillé, or at Innocent's the Pastry-cook, opposite the Painted Wine-vault[1] at Chinon, under penalty of stripping to my Doublet and cooking my little Pasties myself.

" My good Man, couldn't you throw me ashore ?  I will give you all that I have, if you will throw me ashore. Iarus !  Iarus !

"Ah !  my fair Friends, since we cannot make a good Harbour, let us come to anchor in some Road, I know not where.  Drop all your Anchors ; let us be out of this Danger, I beseech you.

" My Friend, heave the Line and the Lead, an't please you.  Let us know how many Fathom we are in.  Take a

---

1 *La Cave peincte* was a *dépen*     sort of cellar in the rock.  *Garg.*
*dance* of the house (*La Lamproie*)     12, v. 35.
of Rabelais' father at Chinon, a

Sounding, my Friend, in the Lord's name. Let us know if
a man could easily drink here bolt upright; I believe he
could and without stooping."

"On this Side ho!" cried Friar John; "in all the
Devils' name. Wait a bit! Draw forth, my Friend; so,
by the Powers! Here is rare hailing and thundering, in
good sooth. Hold hard above there, please."

"Alas!" said Panurge, "Friar John is damning himself
rarely on credit. O what a good Friend I am losing in
him!

"Iarus! Iarus! here it comes worse than ever: we are
going from Scylla to Charybdis,[1] holos! I am drowning.
*Confiteor.* Just one Word by way of a Will, Friar John,
my Father, good Mr. Abstractor,[2] my Friend, my Achates,[3]
Xenomanes, my All. Alas, I am drowning. Two Words
of a Will. Hold here, here on this Stool.

---

1 "Incidis in Scyllam cupiens
vitare Charybdin" occurs in the
*Alexandreïs* of Philippe Gaultier
(Book v., line 301). The notion is,
of course, from Hom. *Od.* xii. 85-
110. Cf. Erasm. *Adag.* i. 5, 4.

2 *Abstractor,* i.e., of Quintes-
sence—Rabelais himself. cf. Title-
page to *Gargantua,* and v. 20.

3 *Achates,* cf. *Pant.* 9, iii. 47.

# CHAPTER X

"To make a Will," said Epistemon, "at this time when
we ought to be bestirring ourselves and helping our Crew,
under penalty of being shipwrecked, seems to me an Act
as unseasonable and unfitting as that of the Subalterns and
Minions of ᵃCaesar as he was coming into Gaul. They a B G. i. 3
busied themselves with making Wills and Codicils, be-
moaned their Fate, bewailed the Absence of their Wives
and Friends in Rome, when of necessity they ought to
have run to Arms and exerted themselves against their
Enemy Ariovistus.

"It is a Folly like that of the Carter who, when his
Waggon was upset in a Stubble-field,[1] on his Knees im-
plored the Help of Hercules, instead of goading his Oxen
and using his Hands to help up the Wheels.

"Wherein will it serve you to make a Will here? For
either we shall escape this Danger or we shall be drowned.

"If we escape it will be of no Service to you. Wills are
of no Value or Authority except by the Death of the
Testators.[2]

---

1 The Fable of the Carter and
Hercules is included in the *Aesopi
Fabulae* of the *Autores Octo
Morales*, cf. *Garg.* 14 It is No. 20
of the collection of Babrius, and is
given in Suidas.

2 Cf. Heb. ix., 17. Testamentum
enim in mortuis confirmatum est,
alioquin nondum valet dum vivit
qui testatus est. Also the legal
maxim : Omne testamentum morte
consummatum est.

"If we are drowned, will it not drown likewise? Who will bear it to the Executors?"

"Some kind Wave," answered Panurge, "will throw it ashore as one did [b]Ulysses; and some Daughter of a King going to sport in the fresh Air will find it, and then will have it carefully executed, and will have some magnificent Cenotaph erected in my Memory near the Shore,

[c]as Dido did to her Husband Sichaeus;

[d]Aeneas to Deiphobus on the Trojan Shore near Rhoeté;

[e]Andromache to Hector in the City of Buthrotum;

[f]Aristotle to Hermeias and Eubulus;

the Romans to [g]Drusus in Germany and to [h]Alexander Severus their Emperor in Gaul;

[i]Catullus to his Brother;

[j]Statius to his Father;

Germain de Brie to Hervé the Breton Captain."[1]

"Art thou doting?" said Friar John. "Help here, help, by five hundred thousand millions of Cartloads of Devils! May the Pox seize on thy Moustaches, and three Rows of Botches, to make thee a Pair of Breeches and a new Cod-piece!

"Is our Ship on a Sandbank? By the Powers, how shall we float her again? What an all-devilish Sea is

b *Od.* v. 425, vi. 85.

c *Aen.* iv. 457.

d *Id.* vi. 505.

e *Id.* iii. 302.

f Diog. L. v. 1 8.

g Suet. v. 1.

h Lamp. *Al. Sev.* 63.

i *Carm.* 110.

j *Silv.* v. 3.

---

1 Germain de Brie (*Germanus Brixius*) composed a poem *Herveii Cenotaphium* on the brave conduct of Hervé de Porzmoguer, who in an engagement with the English off St. Matthieu, Aug. 10, 1513, finding his ship *la Cordelière* fired past saving, grappled with his English opponent *The Regent of England*, so that they both sank together with their crews. Sir T. More made fun of this poem in some epigrams, and Brixius replied in a bitter elegiac poem of 400 lines entitled *Anti-Morus* to which More did not condescend to reply. *Menagiana*, i. 131.

running here ! We shall never escape or I give myself to all the Devils."

Panurge said : " God and the blessed Virgin be with us ! Holos, holos ! I am drowning. Iarus ! *In manus.* Gracious Heaven, send me some ᵏDolphin to carry me safe ashore like a pretty little Amphion.¹ I will play well on the Harp if it be not unstrung."

k Ov. *F.* ii. 83-116.

" I give myself·to the Devil," said Friar John—

" God be with us," said Panurge between his Teeth—" if the Close at Seuillé² had not been lost in this way, if I had done nothing but ¹chant *contra hostium insidias*, as did the other Devils of Monks. instead of succouring the Vine against the Marauders of Lerné."

l *Garg.* 27.

" Land ! Land !" cried Pantagruel ; " I see Land.⁸ Only a Sheep's Courage, my Lads ; we are not far from Harbour. I see the Sky beginning to clear up on the Tramontane side. Look out for the Scirocco !"

" Courage, my Hearties," said the Pilot, "the Sea is abated. Hands aloft to the Fore-top! Helm a-weather!"

" Haul up your Mizzen-topsails !" said Friar John. " Heave aho, my Lads, with all your Might. Heave, heave, heave away !

" 'Tis well said. Methinks the Storm is abating. Our Devils are beginning to scamper to the right-about."

" O," cried Epistemon, " I bid you all be of Good cheer. I see there Castor⁴ on the Right."

---

1 *Amphion*, a mistake for *Arion*, corrected in B.

2 *If the close at Seuillé*, &c. This passage is transposed in B. to a later place in c. 23.

3 Suggested by a remark of Diogenes at a recitation of a long book, when he saw at last a blank page, θαῤῥεῖτε, ἄνδρες, γῆν ὁρῶ. D. Laert. vi: 2, 38. *Terram video.* Erasm. *Ad.* iv. 8. 18.

4 *Castor.* This is known as St. Elmo's fire. St. Erasmus (Ermo, Elmo) was martyrized about 304 at Formies. He was buried at Gaeta, and was supposed to send the double lights which were propitious in a storm. Castor and Pollux represented the twin-lights, and Helen the single one which was feared. Cf. Plin. ii. § 37. Hor. *Od.* i. 3, 2 ; i. 12, 27-32.

"Be, be, bous, bous, bous," said Panurge, "I am mightily afraid it is Helen."

m Plut. *Q. Gr.*
23, 296 F.

"It is verily [m] Mixarchagetas," answered Epistemon, "if you like better the Appellation given by the Argives. Ho! ho! I see Land; I see the Harbour; I see a great Number of people on the Harbour; I see a Light on an Obeliscolychny.[1]  Mind you don't take her in athwart."

"Courage," cried Pantagruel, "Courage, my Lads. Let us shew Courtesy. See here, near our Ship are two Barks and six Frigates, which the good People of this neighbouring Island are sending to our Help.

n Verg. *A.* ii.
312.

"But who is this [n] Ucalegon below there, who cries out so and distresses himself? Did I not hold the Mast firmly with my Hands, and more upright than two hundred Cables could do?"

Friar John answered: "That is the poor Devil Panurge, who has the Calf's Ague; he is quaking for Fear when he is full."

"If," said Pantagruel, "he hath been in Fear during this horrible Coil and perilous Storm, provided that otherwise he hath acted manfully, I do not esteem him a Jot the less for it; for, as it is indicative of a dull and cowardly Heart to fear in every Encounter, as did Agamemnon, whom for that Reason Achilles in his Reproaches insultingly declared

o *Il.* i. 255.

to have the [o] Eyes of a Dog and the Heart of a Deer; so, not to fear when the Case is evidently formidable is a Sign that a man possesses little or no Apprehension.[2]

1 *Obeliscolychnies* are explained in a note in the *briefve declaration* to c. 25 (an explanation of the more obscure terms in the Fourth Book, appended to B) as obelisks with lights on them near the sea-shore.

2 This passage is derived from Aristotle *Eth. Nic.* iii. 7, § 7, probably through Erasmus: Fuerit autem quispiam insanus et doloris sensu vacans, si nihil metuat, neque terrae concussiones, neque fluctus, quemadmodum de Celtis praedicant. *Adagia,* iv. 8. 12. The French *signe de peu ou faulte de apprehension* ought probably to be "signe de *fou.*"

" Now if there is anything in this Life to fear, next to offending God, I will not say that it is Death. I do not wish to enter into the Dispute of Socrates and the Academics. But I affirm that this kind of Death by Shipwreck is to be feared, or nothing is : for according to the Judgement of ᵖHomer it is a Thing that is grievous, hateful and ᵖ *Od.* v. 312. unnatural to perish at Sea. The Reason assigned by the Pythagoreans is that the Soul is Fire and of igneous Substance ; therefore the Man dying by Water, the opposite Element, they are of Opinion (although the contrary is the Truth) that the Soul is entirely extinguished.[1] Indeed Aeneas, in the Storm, by which the Fleet of his Ships was surprised near Sicily, regretted that he had not died by the Hand of the brave Diomed, and declared that those were ᑫthree and four times happy who had perished in the ᑫ Verg. A i. 94 Burning of Troy.

" Here on board there is no one dead, God our Saviour be eternally praised for it. But verily here is a Household badly enough in Disorder. Well, we shall have to repair this Wreck. Take care that we do not run aground."

" Ha, ha !" cried Panurge ; "all goes well ; the Storm is over. I beg you to be so kind as to let me be the first to go ashore.[2] I should like very much to go and attend a little to my private Affairs. Shall I help you again there? Hand me that Rope to coil. I have plenty of Courage, i'faith ; of Fear mighty little—hand it here, my Friend—no,

---

1 *The Reason . . . extinguished.* This passage is omitted in B. for prudential reasons. In *Menagiana,* iii. 66, it is stated that the words *Fatum* and *Fata* were not allowed by the Inquisition.

2 Cingar se prora saltans dispiccat ab alta ;
Tangere gaudet humum, passatas devovet undas.
—Merl. Coc. xii. 309-10

no, not a Jot of Fear.[1]   True it is that that decumane[2]
Wave, that broke over us from Prow to Poop, altered my
Pulse a little."
   " Down with the Sails"—" Ay, ay, Sir."—
   " How now, Friar John, are you doing nothing ?   Is this
the Time for us to be drinking now ?   How do we know
whether St. Martin's running Footman[3] is not brewing us
yet another Storm ?
   " Shall I come again and help you there?   By the Powers,
I do much repent me, though it is too late, that I have
not followed the Teaching of the good [r]Philosophers, who
tell us that to walk by the Sea and to sail near the Shore is
a Thing very safe and delectable ; just as it is to go on foot
when we hold our Horse by the Bridle.   Ha, ha, ha !   By
Heaven all goes well.   Shall I help you any more there ?
Hand me that ; I will do that well or the Devil's in't."
   Epistemon, who had his Hand all flayed inside and
bleeding, from having held on to one of the Cables with
might and main, hearing the Discourse of Pantagruel said :
   "Believe me, my Lord, I had Fear and Fright no less
than Panurge ; but, for all that, I did not spare myself in
helping.
   " I consider that, if indeed Death comes (as it doth) by
fatal and inevitable Necessity, to die in such or such a

[r] Plut. *Q. Con.*
i. 4, 5.

1 Fr. *maille*, cf. Je ne vous
crains pas *maille*.   Villon, *Francarchier*, l. 35.
   2 *Decumane* = huge, monstrous.
The tenth wave was supposed to
be larger than the others, and so
the word was used in other connex-
ions with this meaning. *Decumana
porta, acipenser*, &c. Cf. Erasm.
Ad. iv, 8, 54.

3 I.e., the Devil, who according
to the legend threatened the saint:
" Quocumque ieris vel quaecumque
tentaveris diabolus tibi advers-
abitur," and he kept his word.
Instante jam morte, viso humani
generis hoste, " Quid inquit astas,
cruenta bestia?   Nihil in me
funesti reperies." *Legenda Aurea*,
c. 166.

Manner is partly in the holy Will of God, partly in our own Discretion.[1] Wherefore we ought to implore, invoke, pray, beseech and supplicate Him ; we ought likewise on our Part to do our Endeavour, and to assist them to the Means and Remedy. If I do not speak thereof according to the Decrees of the Vain-babblers (*mathéologiens*), they will pardon me ; I speak therein by Book and Authority.[2] s *Garg.* 15.

"You know what C. Flaminius the Consul[t] said, when by Hannibal's Stratagem he was hemmed in near the Lake of Perusia called Thrasymene : 'My Men,' said he to his Soldiers, 'you must not hope to get out from here by Vows and imploring of the Gods ; by Strength and Manhood it behoves us to escape and make a Way by the Edge of the Sword through the midst of our Enemies.' t *Liv.* xxii. 5.

"Likewise in "Sallust; 'The Help of the Gods is not obtained by idle Vows and womanish Lamentations. By watching, working, striving, all things succeed and come to a good End. If in time of Need and Danger a man is negligent, effeminate and idle, it is in vain that he calls upon the Gods ; they are provoked and wrathful against him.'" u *Cat.* 52, § 29.

"Let the good Ship go,"[3] said Panurge, "all goes well. Friar John is doing nothing there, and he looks on at me here sweating and toiling to help this honest Sailor, first of that Name.[4] Prithee, Mate, I would ask you two Words only—but do not be offended. Of what Thickness are the Planks of this Ship?"

1 *Partly*, &c. changed in B. to " is in the holy Will of God."

2 *And to assist them* . . . . *Authority.* This passage is suppressed in B.

3 Fr. *Vogue la galée.* Cf. *Garg.* 3.

4 *First of that Name.* The sailors of that time were not in good repute.

"They are," answered the Pilot, "two good Fingers thick—do not fear."

"By the Powers," said Panurge, "we are then con-
w Diog. L. i. 8, 5. tinually within two <sup>w</sup>Fingers' Breadth of Death. Is this one of the Nine Joys of Marriage?[1] You do well, Mate, in measuring Danger by the Yard of your Fear. For my part, I have not a Jot of it; my Name is William the Fearless; of Courage I have more than my Share. I do not mean the Courage of a Sheep; I mean a Wolf's Courage, the Assurance of a Bravo,[2] and I fear nothing but—Dangers.[3]

"Good morrow, Gentlemen. Good morrow to you, one and all. You are all heartily welcome and in good time. Let us go ashore. Shall I help you again there? I now
x Diog. L. i. 8, 5. find that the <sup>x</sup>Answer of Anacharsis, the good Philosopher, is true and founded on Reason, who, being asked which Ship seemed to him the safest, replied: *That which is in the Harbour.*"

"By the worthy Frock that I wear," said Friar John to Panurge, "Codling, my Friend, thou hast had Fear without Cause and without Reason; for thy Destiny is not to

---

1 In A. P. F. i. pp. 17-32 is preserved a piece entitled *Les Tene-
bres de mariage* (Lyons 1546) in
which there are *neuf* leçons, each
ending,
  Joly mal an, joly mal an
  En mariage souvent a l'en.
There was also a very popular book
called *Les XV. joyes de mariage.*

2 Cf. Comme ung *meurtrier*
lequel *asseuré* ment. Prognostication des Progn. (1537). A. P. F. v.
229. Cf. Arist. *Rhet.* ii. 5 §§ 13-14.
Juv. xiii. 109.

3 Cf. Villon *Francarchier*, l. 98.
Je ne craignoye que les dangiers.

perish by Water. Thou wilt certainly be hung up high in Air[1] or roasted merrily like a Father."[2]

" Ay, ay," answered Panurge, "but the Devils' Cooks are sometimes out in their Office, and often put on to boil that which was designed for burning, fricaseeing and roasting."

1 Qui doibt pendre ne noye, on gibet flotte bas.
      Cretin, p. 129.

2 Fr. *guaillard comme un père.* Cf. iv. 44, *aises comme pères*, and *Les aises de vie monachale, Pant.* 7.

# CHAPTER XI

## How after the Storm Pantagruel landed on the Islands of the Macraeons

IMMEDIATELY after, we landed at the Port of an Island, which they called the Island of the Macraeons.

The good People of the Place received us with Honour. An old Macrobius—so they styled their High Sheriff—wished to take Pantagruel to the Communal House of the Town, to refresh himself at his Ease and to take his Refection ; but he would not leave the Mole till all his Men were landed.

After having called their Muster, he commanded each one of them to have a Change of Raiment, and all the Ships' Stores to be set out on Land, so that all the Crews could make Good cheer. Which was incontinently done, and God wot how they all drank and regaled themselves. All the People of the Place brought them Victuals in abundance ; the Pantagruelists gave them more in return. True it is that he who hath the most doth not speak of it.

END OF THE FOURTH BOOK

.

www.ingramcontent.com/pod-product-compliance
Lightning Source LLC
Chambersburg PA
CBHW020328090426
42735CB00009B/1445